Super Powers: Reading with Print Strategies and Sight Word Power

Lucy Calkins, Amanda Hartman, and Elizabeth Dunford Franco, with Colleagues from the Teachers College Reading and Writing Project

Photography by Peter Cunningham

Illustrations by Marjorie Martinelli

HEINEMANN ◆ PORTSMOUTH, NH

To Giselle McGee, for putting joy and care at the center, and knowing rigor will follow—Lucy

To Liz Phillips, for reminding us that our field needs leadership and that leadership takes courage—Amanda

To Adele Schroeder, for going to the ends of the earth to give kids the richest possible start—Liz

Heinemann
361 Hanover Street
Portsmouth, NH 03801–3912
www.heinemann.com

Offices and agents throughout the world

The authors and publisher wish to thank those who have generously given permission to reprint borrowed material:

In the Garden. Copyright © 2000 by Harcourt Achieve, Inc. Used by permission of Cengage Australia.

So Much! Text copyright © 1994 by Trish Cooke. Illustrations copyright 1994 © by Helen Oxenbury. Reproduced by permission of the publisher, Candlewick Press.

From *Mouse Has Fun: It's Super Mouse!* Text copyright © 2002 by Phyllis Root. Illustrations copyright © 2002 by James Croft. Reproduced by permission of the publisher, Candlewick Press.

Materials by Kaeden Books and Lee & Low Books, appearing throughout the primary Reading Units of Study series, are reproduced by generous permission of the publishers. A detailed list of credits is available in the Kindergarten online resources.

Cataloging-in-Publication data is on file with the Library of Congress.

ISBN-13: 978-0-325-07700-0

Series editorial team: Anna Gratz Cockerille, Karen Kawaguchi, Tracy Wells, Felicia O'Brien, Debra Doorack, Jean Lawler, Marielle Palombo, and Sue Paro
Production: Elizabeth Valway, David Stirling, and Abigail Heim
Cover and interior designs: Jenny Jensen Greenleaf
Photography: Peter Cunningham
Illustrations: Marjorie Martinelli
Composition: Publishers' Design and Production Services, Inc.
Manufacturing: Steve Bernier

Printed in the United States of America on acid-free paper
19 18 17 16 15   VP   1 2 3 4 5

Acknowledgments

THIS UNIT HAS BEEN a favorite at the Project for many years, and over all those years, it has developed as a pearl does, with one person after another adding layers of insight and imagination. The grain of sand at the unit's nucleus came from Shanna Schwartz, one of the Project's lead K–2 staff developers. Shanna thought of the storyline: *Readers need super powers*. The progression of the unit was drafted and revised in study groups and think tanks that involved many Project staff members, then piloted and revised again, and again.

To write and rewrite this unit certainly took a village! It'd be impossible to thank everyone who has been a part of it. Thanks to Lucy, for leading the study groups that led to the unit, and for helping with the unit's design. Thanks to staff developers who gave graciously of their energy and wisdom. Rachel Rothman's brilliant understanding of phonics is here, as is Valerie Geschwind's hand on the pulse of kindergarten classrooms. Lindsay Mann's devotion to developmentally responsive teaching is here, too. The pages brim with contributions from Natalie Louis (everlastingly spunky and child-centered) and Shanna Schwartz (notice her attentiveness to providing and releasing scaffolds) and Christine Holley (she kept us laughing as we worked). The list goes on and on. Thank you to all the staff developers who contributed their time, ideas, and words to make this the very best unit that it could be.

Thanks to our chief learner and leader, Lucy Calkins. You have led us on a wonderful journey over the years, in creating a kindergarten curriculum. Thank you for teaching us how to strengthen the details of our teaching, for showing us how to write cohesive streamlined units. Thank you for all you do to challenge us, inspire us, and get us to work in the best collaborative ways. This unit exemplifies our collaborative creativity and the grand knowledge that we hold.

To the other leaders at the project: Laurie Pessah, Kathleen Tolan, and Mary Ehrenworth, thank you for all of the support, ideas, and energy you brought not only to this primary team of staff developers but to the organization as a whole. You do so much to hold and lead the community together. Thank you. We would also like to thank our Senior Reading Specialists, Joe Yukish and Cheryl Tyler, for all your input over the years and specifically with this project.

A big thank you and hug to Julia Mooney, our co-writer of all things primary. Thank you for all you have done across the years with this curriculum and specifically with this book. Your beautiful writing and ideas are so appreciated, and we are always too glad to work alongside you.

Thanks to our editors, Jean Lawler and Havilah Jespersen, your attention to detail and careful clarifications and additions to the text. Your time and attention to detail have made this book friendly to teachers and students. Our thanks to Taryn Vanderberg, Anne Marie Johnston, Beth Moore, and Nilaja Taylor for your wise contributions. We also offer a huge thank you to our support team from the Literacy Specialist graduate program: Rebecca Rappaport, Julie Steinberg, and Liz Sherry.

The glorious cover art and design for the book are gifts from the talented Jenny Jensen Greenleaf, our designer. She works with photographs from Peter Cunningham, who has become an integral part of the brand. J. Robert Parks, the photo editor, works with David Stirling, our own superhero. Abby Heim, oversees the entire effort of transforming Google Docs into the gold of these books—and that's an act of magic indeed.

The people who truly make this unit sing, however, are the teachers and kids who breathe their own originality and passion into it. Thanks to all the teachers who have piloted the unit over the years and helped us to clarify the ideas that have finally made it onto these pages. A special thanks to the kindergarten teams at PS 79Q and PS 503K, to Kristi Mraz at PS 59M, a former staff member who sets the world on fire with her teaching, and to Connie Finkelstein, Mia Smith, and Karen Olsen.

—Amanda, Liz, and the entire TCRWP Community

Contents

BEND III   Bringing Books to Life

Read-Aloud and Shared Reading

An Orientation to the Unit

AS YOU ENTER THIS SECOND UNIT, we hope you breathe a little sigh of relief. By now, your children are familiar enough with the daily rhythms and routines of reading workshop that they are beginning to function with greater independence. They may need little nudges here and there, but they know how to move from their seats to the rug and back again, how to choose texts and read them as best they can, and how to sit knee to knee with a partner and enjoy a book together. Your children are beginning to talk with one another about books more easily, and your partnerships work with a hum rather than in spurts and starts. This means that you can confer with a satisfying number of children and meet with flexible small groups for guided reading and strategy lessons.

In the first unit, your students had repeated opportunities to read and reread emergent storybooks, otherwise known as old favorites. Children learned to rely on the pictures and their knowledge of how these stories go to tell the stories, both on their own and with a partner. Perhaps the biggest thing your children took away from the first unit is the fact that they are readers, able to read anything, anywhere in the world. By conveying this message, you will have set the stage for the theme song of this second unit book—that kids are super readers, who can activate lots of "super powers" (strategies) to read with even greater skill!

In this book, you will ramp up the volume of your instruction, now teaching your children to draw on multiple sources of information—meaning, syntax, and the sounds of letters so they can begin to use them at the beginning of the words in level C books. You'll teach children that they can build on the work they've been doing in emergent storybooks, shared reading, and even unfamiliar books, now with increasing independence. Meanwhile, you'll place a greater emphasis on looking at the print and developing the concept of one-to-one matching to help students understand that the print conveys meaning.

Throughout this unit, you will find that many of your students are both able do this work in a shared, highly familiar text and ready to do it in their own books. We often call texts for shared reading big books, though these include enlarged songs, poems, charts, and all sorts of texts that the whole class has studied. In this unit, children will read copies of these familiar, shared texts. As you assess students and match them to just-right reading levels, you'll introduce them to book baggies so that they can continue to read familiar texts, as well as their own just-right books. At this stage in the year, children at benchmark will read emergent storybooks, shared reading texts, and unfamiliar level A and B books. "Unfamiliar" books are ones you've read only once or twice during shared reading (whole group or small group), or books you've introduced to kids, reading just the first few pages before giving them to children to finish on their own.

This unit is organized into three bends. In the first bend, "Using Super Powers to Look and Point, and Then Read Everything," you'll announce that children have "super powers" for reading, and you'll spotlight "pointer power," helping children point as they read familiar texts, using one-to-one matching, tapping each word just once, checking that their reading makes sense, and pointing to words they know "in a snap."

The next bend, "Taking On Even the Hardest Words," rallies kids to use their powers to read, as they move from familiar texts to unfamiliar ones. Children will learn that it helps to use a combination of strategies, not just one isolated strategy at a time, when reading. You'll add to students' repertoire of super powers (reading strategies), teaching them to search for meaning, use picture clues, begin to search visual information, use the sound of the first letter of a word and newly learned snap words, and develop persistence as readers when they feel stuck.

In the final bend, "Bringing Books to Life," you'll invite students to draw on all of their super powers as they read. Children will read both to themselves and to others, working to make their voices smoother (fluency) and to communicate their understanding of the text (meaning). They'll read attending to patterns, end punctuation—and changes in these, and to meaning. Partners will share favorite parts of books during book talks. Throughout this bend, you'll encourage children to draw on all they learned earlier in the year, too: to read smoothly with expression and to fix up any parts that don't look or sound right.

THE INTERSECTION OF READING DEVELOPMENT AND THIS UNIT

At this point in kindergarten, most of your children are still four and five years old; still so young! But they're also brimming with energy and the desire to read. One of the truths about early childhood education that undergird this series is that young children learn through play, through drama, through exploring. This unit is written in a way that echoes that childhood truth. The unit dramatizes the idea that to read, you call on super powers, just like superheroes do. The joy and playfulness of this overarching structure is the biggest idea of the unit, and also one of the biggest ideas of early childhood teaching and learning.

This unit, therefore, will work well when it is playful—not "This is how you read" but instead "Oh, my gosh, we have to use our super-strength, extra-special powers to read this book!" Equally important is the message that "Superheroes don't give up in a jam!" That spirit is already within your children, too—when things are hard, if they can be playful, they persist. You will want to bring a fun-loving spirit to the unit, sending the message that reading is not a tough job, but joyful. In that spirit, your children can play their way through the new learning they'll take on.

This is also the age where your children are begging anyone and everyone to "Read it again!" They can read the same text a hundred times over, and that eagerness to reread beloved texts characterizes the kinds of work you'll do with them and the kinds of material you'll use. You can make dramatic strides with kids by having them practice their reading super powers with highly familiar materials—books you've read over and over, songs you've sung over and over, charts you've made together and read over and over. Your kindergartners' introduction to paying attention to print, then, is with the highly familiar, where they can bring their characteristic energy and enthusiasm to the task, as they work on concepts about print, such as one-to-one matching.

Of course, some of your children will be reading more conventionally already. Kindergarten always includes a wide range of children and abilities, and even at this stage of the year you are still getting to know your children. This unit can therefore be quite flexible—you can use your super powers to play your way through higher-level books, too, just as you can use your super powers to tell when a word starts and ends. Even if some of your children are strong readers, though, they are still four- and five- year-olds, and they still will benefit from the playful and concrete—touching pictures, dramatizing books.

Your children are in a stage of life where the world is all about them. Spending time with kindergartners, you've undoubtedly heard the phrase "Look at me!" more times than you can count. Your children want you to watch them put on a show, climb on a jungle gym, play a game on an iPad. This unit honors that kindergarten inclination. You'll give your kids lots of chances to show off their newest reading powers and give the gift of reading to those they love and want attention from. Much of kindergarten is helping your children learn social skills—how to read with a partner, how to share, how to function in a group—and many moments in this unit, as is true throughout our kindergarten units, invite kids to make social connections that are about reading and words.

Ultimately, this unit explicitly invites your children into conventional reading. As you move from the land of oral language to the land of symbolic language, you're helping children as they begin trying to map symbols onto pictures and words. This is challenging, exhilarating work, but the part that will make this so powerful for kindergartners at this stage in the year is to hold on to the joyfulness. The world sometimes feels like it's saying that reading is serious business, hard work, and that there's no time for joy and play in children's lives. But as your four- and five-year-olds sing and play in their books, their kindergarten spirits constantly remind us: Joy matters.

OVERVIEW

Bend I: Using Super Powers to Look and Point, and Then Read Everything

One of the most important things to consider, as you launch this first part of this unit, is that your students can already do so much. There are probably many things in the classroom that students can read. This is not only important for you to know but it is also important for your children to know. Your children can probably read some of their classmates' names—names are the first things that many children learn to read. In your word study time so far this year, you have probably done some variation on Pat Cunningham's name study—and even if you haven't, there probably are names throughout the room: at tables, on lockers, on the word wall, on center charts, attendance charts, and so on. You might launch this unit by saying, "Readers, ever since the first day of school, I've watched your reading muscles grow, and grow, and *grow*! Just like that carrot seed grew in our favorite book! Will you look around our classroom right now, and find something that you can read? Maybe it's a sign, or a label, or a chart, or the title of a book. Find something and go stand next to it!"

What a great assessment for you to see what students think that they can read and what a realization for them that they are already reading things in the classroom! Celebrate what they know and then introduce the idea that the reading they've just done shows that, lo and behold, they must hold some sort of reading power! It will be their own work, then, that leads you to think of them as reading superheroes. You may say, "Whoa! I am totally amazed. You guys are the kinds of readers who can just look at a word, point at it, and *read* it. It's almost like you have *super powers* to read everything! You know, I had a feeling this class was special when you walked in here on the first day of school—but I had *no* idea I had a class full of *super readers*!"

After this first discovery that your children are super readers, you will show them new super powers: pointer power, partner power, rereading power! These, of course, translate into the reading behaviors and skills that your children need most. To help move readers towards more conventional reading, you will show them how to match their reading voices with the print on the page. Developing one-to-one matching is one of the early reading behaviors that will help students move into more conventional reading. You will also garner up their spirit to reread, both to support their understanding of what they are reading and also to help them work on their one-to-one matching. As children reread, trying to point to the word as they say it, they'll rely in part on their knowledge of high-frequency words. These will serve as reliable anchors to the sea of words in a sentence.

Songs and chants are staples in our early childhood classroom settings. Use them for literacy. Sing them to gather students to the meeting area and invite the children who are already in the meeting area to read and sing them, too (thus turning those songs into readable materials). You may want to invite your students to not just reread their books but to invent fun and creative ways to do it! You could say to them, "Will you reread with a beat or sing it?" Tapping your leg and singing a line out loud, you could add, "Or will you read in another kind of special voice? Thumbs up when you have a plan." Of course, as you send children off to work, you'll want to ramp up the super power theme: "Ready? Set! Reread power, *activate!*"

Your children will quickly realize they can read not only songs and familiar shared reading books but also copies of charts and signs in the classroom. As the unit unfurls, you'll bring in new familiar texts, and as children demonstrate readiness, you'll channel them to read unfamiliar texts if they can. As children read, one important tool will be a personalized pointer. You'll see that in this unit, you don't just distribute little Popsicle stick pointers as if they are marker pens or any other bit of regular old classroom equipment. No way! In this unit, Reader-Man visits your classroom and leaves your class a note:

"My friend Spider-Man told me that you have been using reading super powers to read *everything* around you. I have a *mega important* tip for you. Sometimes there are lots of words or longer words and you *must* check that you're reading those words correctly. I left you special power pointers, by the sink, to give you even stronger pointer power! When you read, make sure you point one time under each word to make your reading matches the words on the page. Enjoy reading today and every day! Readerly yours, Reader-Man"

Your students will be over the moon. You will see their engagement in books rise, and you will also see their attention to print change as well! To round out this bend, you will want to put these pointers to good use. Students can use them with their partners as you teach them that echo reading is another way to work together. Students can use them to work on long or short words and to use their snap words as anchors. When their pointers are on a word they know, they should make sure that they are saying the right word, or you'll remind them to go back and reread so they try and make the word they say match the letters they see.

All along, you will want to show students how their work is paying off and to play into the drama of their new found powers. "Super Readers, mission accomplished!" As you move on to the next part of the unit, you will want to be introducing a few new super powers, or reading strategies, all the while working on not giving up as well. Let's face it, building student confidence and resilience while reading probably makes as much difference to their development as does teaching students any one reading strategy!

Bend II: Taking On Even the Hardest Words

As you kick off this bend, you will want your students to know that sometimes when they read they will run into trouble. Things will get hard. So you will want to tell them this, right up front: "Super Readers, I've been studying lots of superheroes—Spider-Man, Batman, Supergirl, Wonder Woman, even Reader-Man. And the thing I have found is that each one of them has *power*, yes; but also, each one of them runs into a ton of trouble." You might ask your students to think about whether that seems true to them, and to think about the sorts of difficulties those superheroes encounter and the decisions they make in response. This helps to honor the difficulties that your readers will run into so that instead of trying to hide the words they can't figure out, they will feel empowered to try something—anything! So, ask your students, "When your superhero encounters trouble, does he or she say, 'Oh, dear, that's too hard for me? I better just go hide.' Or does your superhero tackle the trouble?"

You will probably have some conventional readers in your classroom, who are reading levels C and above. You may also have some readers just on the cusp of conventional reading, who are able to read level A/B books and, with some support, can read level C. The rest of your readers are probably emergent readers. If they came into the year hardly knowing their letters and sounds, they'll be reading and working on level A/B texts and other familiar texts (like charts, songs, and shared reading books). The truth is, for all your readers, the big books you have read during shared reading and the songs and nursery rhymes your class is coming to know by heart make for great reading materials. You will want to be sure, though, that readers who are reading conventionally also have a slew of just-right books. The strategies you'll support in whole-class instruction, such as one-to-one matching, using snap words to anchor reading, and not giving up when they encounter difficulty, will be useful for *all* of the readers in your classroom because no matter where readers are in the level progression, it'll be important for them to track print (with their fingers or eyes), figure out the words, and increase the number of high-frequency words they know in a snap.

Drawing readers' attention to the words on the page will be helpful, but as they pay attention to words, be sure your readers don't forget to also draw information from the pictures in their books. In most of your children's books, the pictures will support their understandings of the text. "If your partner starts to feel defeated, you can help by giving your partner some picture power! Tap the picture for your partner. Point to the thing in the picture that might help. Remind your partner to use not only pointing power but also picture power," you'll say. Partners can be like teachers. They don't have to give answers to the child who is reading, but rather, they can coach, much like teachers do.

Pictures are especially helpful when readers use them even before they run into trouble. To help readers be successful on their first try reading a page, encourage them to first preview the book and, indeed, the page. "Readers, another way to use your picture power is to use it *before* you get into trouble! You know that you can practice using picture power *before* you read the page and see if that helps you *avoid* trouble!"

Throughout the day, you are giving your students many opportunities to learn how to read and write and put the parts of literacy together. For example, during word study, you will teach your students high-frequency words that they can in turn use while they read and write in workshop. In this *Super Powers* unit, you not only teach new words but also how children can teach *themselves* new words. In this part of the unit, you give students the same exact steps you use during word study.

1. **Look** at the word.
2. **Read** the word.
3. **Spell** the word.
4. **Write** the word.
5. **Look** at the word.
6. **Read** the word.

This process will help your readers in multiple ways. Not only does it help them learn new words so that they can use these words as anchors but it will also help them to see that what we do in one part of the day can be used all day long. The skills children are learning in the writing workshop will be super important during reading time. You can point out that the spaces between words that they are learning about during the writing workshop are already made for them in their books. They just need to move their pointing finger accordingly as they read, hopping from word to word.

To help students make these links and transfer their skills from one part of the day to the next, you'll want to do some interactive writing with them.

During interactive writing, they can work on making spaces between words, using their alphabet charts, forming letters, creating patterns, using high-frequency words, and more! You may want your students to actually write about superheroes (the theme of this unit) in their own, homemade A/B level texts. "Let's start by thinking about who we can write about. Hmm, maybe it can go like this: Look at Superman fly. Look at Wonder Woman run. How could the next page go?" In that example, page one says '*Look* at Superman fly.' for a reason. *Look* is a snap word. You can recruit children to find *look* on the word wall. "Shout out the letters," you can say, as they scan the world wall.

It will be important to make sure your students are using more letter sounds in their writing now, labeling their pictures with first and final sounds, and sometimes writing sentences in which they make spaces between their words. They should be moving to a place where they are able to really read back their own writing, using one-to-one matching.

In reading, too, be sure that you are supporting and teaching your students to use those letter sounds that they have been learning and using in writing. While this is not the emphasis in this unit, it is still a good idea to begin to introduce it here, early in the year. Remember, you have a range of readers in your classroom. Learning how to use the letters will be something that may take time and a lot of practice for your kids. Start now. You can return to this in small groups or one-to-one conferences. This focus will reappear and be front and center in the next unit as well.

The last power you will introduce in this bend is certainly something you have been working on since the beginning of this unit, and that is persistence power! You want to make sure that even as students try this power, they know they can try different strategies, too. This is really the idea of becoming a flex-ible word solver—-one who integrates all sources of information. It is also an ethos to build into your curriculum, all day long. Research shows that those who are willing to persist and to show grit in times of difficulty find more success. Others who quickly give up generally remain stuck and unchanged. This isn't to say that as readers persist they will always get it; rather, they are more likely to move ahead because they are activating their own agency in their work. You might say, "I have something else important to tell you, readers. We know that persistence power can be used when you get stuck and have to figure out a hard word. But sometimes, readers think they've defeated a hard word and then realize that something is not quite right. When that happens, readers can use persistence power to fix it up. Did this happen for any of you as you read today? Thumbs up if you activated your persistence power!"

You will end this bend with a mini celebration. This will help students recognize their recent achievement and be able to show off some of what they have learned. You will want students to think about how they can use their powers together. You may even want them to gather up a couple of goals to work on. Maybe you get them to affix their goal (a quick symbol or letter that represents the powers they are working on) to their tables as reminders. Then after they have read and shown off their powers to their partners, you might create a playful ceremony that honors all their hard work and attention to get-ting stronger as readers. Perhaps you will say, "You rank right up there with Spider-Man, Supergirl, Wonder Woman, and Reader-Man … with all of the superheroes! You have earned your capes!" Then you might either give each child a super reader cape that you have constructed out of construction paper or fabric, or you could invite each child to make his or her own, decorating these with glitter, felt, buttons—the works.

Bend III: Bringing Books to Life

For this final bend you will want to focus on helping your readers bring their reading to life, rereading their books with more fluency, expression, and even a little drama. As they start to read with more meaning, you'll encourage them to retell their books to each other and to talk about those books, too. While these books are not the deepest, nor are they the most exciting books in the world to talk about, you do want your students to have fun together talking about what's happened in the book that they have just read a zillion times. Retelling is a major skill that will only become more complicated as children read more complex texts, so now is a good time to begin to work on it.

You might, at the end of the first lesson in this bend, channel your readers to practice reading with a bit more fluency, helping beginning readers scoop up a few more words at a time when rereading familiar texts in order to read more smoothly. "Super Readers, with all those reading powers you have, you can bring everything you read to life! Don't let those books, poems, songs, or charts down by reading them in a boring or choppy way. Take out what you brought with you from your baggie. Turn in towards your reading partners and take turns reading to each other, making your voice sound just like mine when I read to you. Ready? Go!" Then you can send your children off to their reading spot by saying, "Super Readers, it is clear that you are ready to take on this great responsibility of bringing your books to life, when you read to someone *and* when you read to yourself."

When students read the following text, many of them will recognize that Super Mouse keeps jumping off things, and they'll have great predictions about what will happen on the next page.

It's Super Mouse!
Super Mouse jumps off a step.
Super Mouse jumps off a box.

One student predicted, "I think he's going to jump off a car!" Another said, "Yeah, or the roof!" When you see that your students have done the "thinking work" of recognizing the pattern, then you can draw their attention back to the words: "So how will the next page go? Say it like the book. Super Mouse …" Some kids might say, "Super Mouse jumps off a car!" "Super Mouse jumps off a roof!"

You'll also teach your children to pay attention to the punctuation on the page. Ending punctuation, the period, is the last concept, number 13, on the Concepts about Print assessment. To introduce this to your students, you might tell them about driving on the road, paying attention to all the traffic signs that tell you to slow down or to stop. You could bring photographs of road signs and traffic lights and say, "These signs and lights are almost like a secret code for drivers, letting them know what to do and how to drive." Then you let children know that punctuation acts in the same way for readers.

Finally, as you come towards the end of this bend and the unit as a whole, you will want to teach two final things. The first thing is that readers have book talk power, and the second thing is that readers retell what happened in their books.

At the end of the unit, during the celebration, your children can give the gift of reading to a special someone. Ask each child to choose a book he or she loves and to choose the person who will receive the gift. Will it be their mom, their sister, the teacher who supervises them at recess, the principal? You will explain this celebration to kids by saying something like, "People have been reading to you for all of your life. Now that *you* are reading, you can give the gift of reading to someone else!" Whomever they choose, the work of the day is to get their reading ready to perform, and the performance will be the gift. Students will have time to rehearse and practice with partners, giving each other tips to improve the reading. You can add to this by showing students that they can add gestures and acting to their reading. At the end of workshop, students can work in small groups, serving as the first audience for each other's gift of reading. These groups function as just one last rehearsal before children give the gift to their selected person.

ASSESSMENT

Conduct some follow-up assessments to the ones you used in the previous unit of study.

Certainly, at the start of this unit, you will want to return to your Concepts about Print assessment to identify which concepts your students still need to work on. You will also want to see how many letter names and sounds your students know with automaticity. Usually by the end of the fall and early winter, most kindergartners know all of their letter names and sounds.

During reading workshop, you will be searching for signs of children who demonstrate these early reading behaviors. You'll watch for children who are working on pointing to words and making a one-to-one match as they read. Look for children who are trying to carry the pattern from one page to the next. Look for signs that children know some letter sounds, especially consonants (vowels typically come later). Be ready to celebrate these signs of progress.

One of the most important places to look for signs of reading progress will be in your students' writing. Their writing will give you an instant sense of what each student knows about print, and this can allow you to determine which children are probably ready for conventional reading (level C and above). The rule of thumb is that if you can read quite a bit of the child's writing, then chances are that child is ready to read at least level C books. That is, if the child is writing with beginning and ending sounds (and some medial sounds) and leaving spaces between words, chances are that child is able to read conventionally. Another way to say this is that you can look to see which children in your class are using a few letters and sounds in their labels or sentences, are making spaces between words, and can read their writing to you (or parts of it). If your students have all three of these things, you will probably want to conduct a running record.

Decide who is ready and conduct a formal running record.

Many of your students will have mastered eleven or twelve of the concepts about print and will know most of their letter names and sounds, so you will definitely want to conduct a running record to set the next goals. To learn more about running records, you can refer to Chapter 6 in *A Guide to the Reading Workshop, Primary Grades*.

After you have conducted the running record, end with a teaching point that comes out of what you noticed about the child as a reader; this can be an on-the-spot, data-based conference. A quick assessment can give you the information you need to either move a child into leveled texts right away (providing an individual book baggie with just-right books) or to plan out how you will confer and conduct small-group work for that child.

At levels A and B when you conduct a running record, remember you will not be looking for accuracy, but instead will want to see how students are using pictures and one-to-one matching to read the words on the page. Also, you will not just aim to assess a student's just-right reading level, you will also want to do a running record at the next level up to identify a few reading goals.

Track to see that your students are growing and changing throughout the year. Many kindergartners who end the year at benchmark levels read level A/B books by November, with a book introduction. By January, most read B/C books, with a book introduction.

If you have been teaching *Super Powers: Reading with Print Strategies and Sight Word Power* and most of your children do not yet have one-to-one matching, rather than moving into Unit 3 (*Bigger Books, Bigger Reading Muscles*), you may want to extend this unit for another two weeks, so that your children are primed to take advantage of Unit 3, which is ideally suited to readers who are ready to read books at level C and above. Further, if your students need more support recognizing letter-sounds, or more support with emergent storytelling, there is a unit in the online resources of *If … Then … Curriculum: Assessment-Based Instruction, Grades K–2*, titled "Emergent Reading: Looking Closely at Familiar Texts."

For more information about our running records, early assessments, and benchmark charts, visit our website at http://readingandwritingproject.org/resources/assessments/running-records.

Gather more information about your students who are becoming more conventional readers.

For students who are beginning to read leveled texts, you may also decide to conduct a spelling inventory and high-frequency word list assessment to identify features of phonics and high-frequency words to continue to introduce and teach. To learn more about these assessments, you can go to Chapter 6 in *A Guide to the Reading Workshop, Primary Grades*.

GETTING READY

Gather books, poems, charts, songs, and more for your students to read.

One of the most important things you can do to successfully teach children to read is to provide them with texts that they'll have success reading. Before you start this unit, it will be important for you to fill book tubs with familiar texts and place them on the tables. Children will read those texts during both private and partner reading times.

Hopefully you have small copies of some favorite big books, especially ones that are repetitive and catchy and easy for students to read, such as *Brown Bear, Brown Bear* and *Mrs. Wishy Washy* and *I Went Walking*. Poems, nursery rhymes, and songs that the class knows by heart will be perfect. You will also want to include copies of well-known charts or tools, such as your class name chart, an alphabet chart, and small copies of your word wall words (scaled down to fit on one page or on cards fastened by a ring).

In addition, we suggest you and your class co-create texts during shared or interactive writing and then make little copies of those texts to add to your tubs so that those books become reading material for your kids. You will already have some class books from the first unit, but plan to create many more quickly—during morning meeting, math, social studies, or any time throughout the day. These books might contain five to seven pages. One may be called "Our Trip to the Bakery" (if the class took such a trip), or "Things We Like to Do." You may decide to use photographs as the picture supports, or you might set up a center during choice time to have different children draw pictures that represent each page. The pictures might contain five or so labels that you and your kids write together, such as *sun, school, bus, kids,* or *tree*. Children can use pointers to locate and read the labels on those pages. Of course, there will also be a sentence on each page, and children can read that as well (perhaps with help). Given that many classroom teachers begin to add high-frequency words to the word wall each week, we suggest using those words in the class books that you author together, creating patterned texts so that students have the support of repetition and predictability when reading. For example, one page could read, "We like to …" and subsequent pages would repeat the pattern.

If your children have published any of their own books, made during the writing workshop, then by all means, those books can go into the tubs as well.

You may also decide to turn labels around the room into phrases or sentences. If earlier, you labeled the classroom door "door," now you might revise the label so it reads "the door." Then, you could make a sentence: "This is the door" or "See the door" or "Look at the door." These will also make wonderful reading materials to use during the reading workshop, with children being invited to take a pointer and read the room.

Match the texts with the reading skills your students are working on.

Your goal during this unit is to have children not only practice concepts of print but also "read" with one-to-one matching, so you will want to steer children toward simple level A and B books. Begin doing this as you progress through Bend I, gradually transitioning your readers into individual book baggies. Start with the readers who are beginning to read conventionally, using a running record to assess each child's starting reading level, and then supply that child with leveled books in addition to some familiar texts from your tubs. By the time you begin your second bend, most (and probably all) of your students should at least be able to gesture towards reading level A books with one-to-one matching. If you think some of your readers should be spending all their time reading familiar texts, by the start of Bend II you will probably want to take those familiar texts out of the tubs and put them into baggies for those readers who are not yet reading conventionally, so their work looks like the work that others are doing.

Ideally, you will have given children introductions to all of the leveled books that go into their baggies. There are a few ways you might pull this off. We recommend you read aloud a few leveled books each day, perhaps as part of a teaching share, morning meeting, choice time, or even a quick small group. In much of the small group work in this unit, children also work in texts you have introduced. These books can be added to their book baggies after the small group, once they can handle the texts successfully. You might also carry some leveled books with you as you confer, using this as another opportunity to introduce new texts. A simple read-aloud or a quick book introduction can accomplish two goals: familiarizing children with the sound of the text and vocabulary, and enticing children to want to read the books you have shared. Aim to build up excitement around these little leveled books, so that children exclaim, "I want to read that one!"

You also can invite parent volunteers or older students who are book buddies into your classroom at this point in the year and show them how to do simple book introductions. A perfect book introduction is not easy to pull off, but this may not be a time for perfection!

Select and gather books and texts for minilessons and guided reading.

You will want to gather some books and texts to use in your minilessons. Select some songs or chants that your students know well. Have on hand both an enlarged copy that you can read together, as well as smaller copies that students could read with a partner during the active engagement. Songs like The Itsy-Bitsy Spider and possibly your clean up song will work well. We also suggest using a couple different leveled texts in Bends II and III. You might start with a level B text, such as *In the Garden* by Annette Smith, Beverley Randell, and Jenny Giles, a Rigby PM Reader (although there is nothing critical about that one text). As a second leveled text, you might stick with a level B or perhaps one level higher, depending on where most of your class is as readers. We suggest using *It's Super Mouse* by Phyllis Root because it has a highly repetitive pattern, there is a fun character to talk about, and it will be a notch above where more typical kindergartners read in the late fall/ early winter.

You will also want to gather texts to use in your guided reading and shared reading small groups. Choose and select a text one level above your students' just-right book level. For some of your students, that will mean a level A or B book that is unfamiliar to them, and by the end of the unit, it might be a level C book. Many teachers enjoy using the PM reader books and Brand New Readers as beginning books for students to tackle. Use your running records to determine if you have children in your class who read at any other levels. If you do, you will want to gather guided reading books at these levels as well, to assist readers on developing the reading process in leveled, unfamiliar books.

Create and prepare special tools to distribute.

For this unit, you will want to set up some basic tools for your students to use. For starters, you will be introducing each of them to their own book baggies (or containers) that they will use for the rest of the year to hold the books/ texts that they want to read throughout the week.

You will also have large and small copies of interactive writing books that you have made with the class as well as songs, poems, nursery rhymes, and chants that you teach your students.

Lastly, you will want to make sure to give each student some sort of special pointer in Bend I. Some teachers use tongue depressors; others purchase finger flashlights (http://www.amazon.com/40-Super-Bright-Finger-Flashlights/dp/B0018LAGZY). Whatever you decide, you will want the pointer to be thin and small enough for students to be able to use as they read their own books to help them engage in one-to-one matching.

During word study, you will introduce high-frequency words to your class and then record these on your word wall. In this unit, you will use your word wall to teach students how to use anchor words (such as *the*) to help them read. You will also teach them how to learn new words as they read, using the same methods that you use when you introduce words on your word wall. You will therefore want to make sure that students have tools to practice this work, both with you and on their own. Some teachers start a word ring of these words for students to keep in their book baggies throughout the year.

READ-ALOUD AND SHARED READING

Use the read-aloud plan at the back of this book to prepare for one read-aloud across a couple of days, as well as others, across the unit.

For this unit, we selected *So Much* by Trish Cooke as the read-aloud text. At the back of this book, you will find a read-aloud section where we have written out a script for think-alouds, listening prompts, and turn-and-talks that you may want to do with your students. You will also see that in your Resource Kit you have yellow Post-it notes with the prompts written on them, which you can directly transfer into your own copy of the book. We hope that this will help cut back on your planning time, giving you more time to study and think about your students' work. We imagine that you will then be able to remove these Post-it notes and use them in another read-aloud text that you select. All of the prompts are transferable across texts.

Select books that are engaging and have complex stories that will be fun to talk and think about.

There are several reasons why we chose *So Much* as this unit's read-aloud text. For starters, we chose a picture book that features engaging characters and strong story language, much like the emergent story books you read across the last unit. Reading aloud exposes children to richer literature than the texts they are able to read independently. While your *shared* reading is aimed

to give students access to texts just a notch above their independent reading level, your *read-aloud* should expose young readers to texts that are much more complex. This text is a level I, a level well above your students' reading levels. It will bring rich vocabulary and a sense of story to your class. We also selected this book because it celebrates the love of family, something young children will quickly relate to. The rhythm of the text quickly hooks listeners as they meet all the aunts and uncles and cousins and grandparents who love the baby *so much*. You'll probably notice that children will chime in as you read the repetitive phrases across the story. This story will easily become a favorite and one that you'll reread time and time again across the month and the year.

Select other types of texts you may want to read aloud.

You might choose to pair your picture book read-aloud with information texts to create a text set, perhaps one that is also linked to your content area study in science or social studies. This can be any book in your library that you love and think is worth using. For example, you might have the popular Todd Parr books, such as, *It's Okay to Be Different* and *The Family Book*. These can help you continue your focus on families, a topic that many kindergarten classrooms start off the school year studying during social studies. While both are patterned list books, they're written at a text level that will be above *most* if not *all* of your readers. These texts will also generate a lot of discussion. You can use these books to build similar skills as well as to deepen students' understanding of themselves and their families. In any case, you, too, can choose and select a series or group of books by the same author or on the same topic that will allow students to not only work on similar skills but also build content around a topic.

Use the five-day plan, in the back of this book, to help you prepare for shared reading.

After the read-aloud template, in the back of this book, you will find a five-day plan for shared reading. We chose to develop a plan for *Brown Bear, Brown Bear, What Do You See?* by Bill Martin Jr. and Eric Carle. This plan is meant to be a template for how you can echo the teaching in this unit of study across a few days. Our hope is that you use this template to replicate the teaching with several other shared reading texts that you select for the remaining weeks of your unit.

Select books that will teach the main skills that echo your unit of study and what your students need as readers.

We selected *Brown Bear, Brown Bear, What Do You See?* for several reasons. One reason we chose this book is that it is a wildly popular and well-known text by many four- to six-year-olds. It has not only engaging pictures but also an engaging rhythm and pattern that students love to sing to and reread often. This text is a level C. If most of your readers are in the emergent stage of reading, then this text will offer a lot of good work, both to develop concepts about print (such as one-to-one matching) and to support the behaviors that readers need in level A/B and C texts.

ONLINE DIGITAL RESOURCES

A variety of resources to accompany this and the other Kindergarten Units of Study for Teaching Reading are available in the Online Resources, including charts and examples of student work shown throughout *Super Powers*, as well as links to other electronic resources. Offering daily support for your teaching, these materials will help you provide a structured learning environment that fosters independence and self-direction.

To access and download all the digital resources for the Kindergarten Units of Study for Teaching Reading:

1. Go to **www.heinemann.com** and click the link in the upper right to log in. (If you do not have an account yet, you will need to create one.)
2. **Enter the following registration code** in the box to register your product: RUOS_GrK
3. Under **My Online Resources**, click the link for the ***Kindergarten Reading Units of Study***.
4. The digital resources are available in the upper right; click a file name to download. (For any compressed ("ZIP") files, double-click the downloaded file to extract individual files to your hard drive.)

(You may keep copies of these resources on up to six of your own computers or devices. By downloading the files you acknowledge that they are for your individual or classroom use and that neither the resources nor the product code will be distributed or shared.)

Using Super Powers to Look and Point, and Then Read Everything

BEND I

Readers Have Super Powers to Look and Point, and Then Read Everything They Can!

IN THIS SESSION, you'll teach children that they can use "super powers" to help them read, starting with the power of pointing under each word to read what it actually says.

GETTING READY

✔ Put an enlarged version of the class name chart front and center and have a pointer ready to summon kids by name (see Connection).

✔ Choose a few printed words in the room (we use the bookshelf label and the names of the week on the classroom calendar), visible to children from their rug spots, that you and students will read aloud (see Teaching).

✔ Make sure a basket of class books ("Things Our Class Likes to Do," "Things Our Class Likes to Eat," "Things Our Class Likes to Play") is prominently displayed for when you challenge children to read more things in the classroom (see Active Engagement).

✔ Place a tub of familiar texts including copies of shared reading books, songs, poems, alphabet charts, name charts, copies of word wall words, and texts written as a class on each table for children to choose items to read (see Link).

✔ Jot on chart paper the words to a "Super Reader" theme song (to the tune of the Spider-Man theme song; see the link, http://vimeo.com/94555464, in the online resources (see Share).

✔ Prepare the chart by placing the heading—"We Are Super Readers!"—and the first strategy Post-it®—"We have pointer power."—onto a sheet of chart paper (see Link).

✔ Take out the strategy Post-it—"We have reread power."—to add to the chart. This chart will be this unit's anchor chart (see Mid-Workshop Teaching).

✔ Revise the "Readers Read with a Partner" chart from Unit 1, *We Are Readers!* Remove three strategy Post-its—"Sit side-by-side," "Share your Wow! pages," and "Reread to learn more" (see Transition to Partner Time).

✔ Take out the strategy Post-it—"Give reminders to use POWERS."—so you can add it to the "Readers Read with a Partner" chart (see Transition to Partner Time).

MINILESSON

CONNECTION

Gather students to the meeting area with a familiar gathering song.

To the tune of "Frère Jacques," I sang the class gathering song, as children chimed in to sing along:

> "We are gathering.
> We are gathering
> On the rug,
> On the rug.
> Everyone is here now,
> finding their own space now.
> We are here.
> We are here."

Once everyone had settled in their spots, I began the lesson.

Celebrate students' growth as readers by inviting them to read around the room, pointing to and reading words they know on charts, labels, or books.

"Readers, ever since the first day of school, I've watched your reading muscles grow, and grow, and grow! Just like that carrot seed grew in our favorite book!

"Will you look around our classroom right now, and find something that you can read? Maybe it's a sign or a label or a chart or the title of a book. Find something and go stand next to it!" The children scattered around the room.

Standing in the middle of the classroom by the enlarged class name chart, pointer in hand, I said, "When I read your name, will you read your sign or label or chart, loud and clear so we can all hear, then go back to your rug spot?" I pointed to *Sara*, the first name on our chart. "Sara!" I read. "Sara, read your sign and then go back to the rug!"

She read, "Sink!"

I nodded. "Give Sara a silent cheer with your hands," I said, doing this to demonstrate. This time, before pointing to another name, I said, "Will you *shout* out the name of our next reader when I point to it? You ready? Watch my pointer carefully. Then, that person, will you do as Sara did and *read* your sign or label or chart and go quickly to your rug spot! Are you ready? We are going to do it quickly. Watch my pointer carefully and get ready to shout out the name."

I then moved through the list of names, with each student in turn reading some bit of environmental print, receiving a silent cheer, and then returning to his rug spot. I proceeded super quickly, and soon the class had gathered, one by one, in the meeting area.

Once the entire class had regrouped, I celebrated their reading growth. "Wow! You can read *so, so* many words. *And* you read this *whole* chart of names, too! Whoa! I am totally amazed. You guys are the kinds of readers who can just look at a word, point at it, and *read* it." I stared wide-eyed at the class. "It's almost like you have *super powers* to read everything! You know, I had a feeling this class was special when you walked in here on the first day of school, but I had *no* idea I had a class full of *Super Readers*!" The children giggled, some flexing their muscles.

❖ Name the teaching point.

"Today I want to teach you that you can use your super reading powers to *actually* read words. You can put your finger under one word, then the next, and the next, and you can *actually read* what the words say."

TEACHING

Celebrate that the class just read the words on the name chart. Suggest that the library alone is filled with words that can be read similarly, by pointing and reading.

"We did that with our name chart, didn't we? I pointed under each name and you actually *read* each name. Let's use that super power—let's call it *pointer power*—even more right now.

"Look at this library area. There are so many things right here that we can read! Watch how I look for even more words to read. When I decide to read a word, I look at the word carefully and put my finger under it and read it.

"Hmm, . . . what should I read first? Oh, here's one." I pointed under a label on the bookshelf beside me. "Okay, watch how I put my finger under the word—not on top of it or next to it. Now I'm going to *actually read* this word. Will you read it with me?"

As you'll see, this particular spin works if you and the kids have been studying the name chart, doing a shared reading of it, and perhaps engaging in Name Study work as described in the Guide.

FIG. 1–1 Two partners frame sight words in a class poem.

You may note that the pronouns are different in this unit. Generally we teach kids what skilled readers do and speak of those readers as "they." In this unit, we talk about what Super Readers can do and address that directly to the kids, as "you, Super Readers." That's because the unit focuses on how kids can do some work that adult readers actually do with automaticity, so it would be a stretch to say this is what skilled adult readers do. Adults no longer point under words and say them one by one, for example.

The class chimed in as we read the label together. "Bookshelf!"

"Now I am going to find something else! The more I use this super power, the *stronger* I'll become. Ready to get stronger with me?" I flashed a muscle pose and the kids flashed one back. "Oh, I spot something else we can use pointer power to read." I walked over to the classroom calendar. "The days of the week! This is a bunch of words—seven words! I'll read the first, and then maybe you can help and we can read the rest together. Okay, here I go. I read, '/M/onday.'"

Then I signaled and said, "Read with me," and together, the class and I read the remaining days of the week aloud.

Debrief, naming what you have done in a way that is replicable and can be done with another word, another time.

"Did you see how I put my finger right under each word, one word at a time, and actually *read the word*? I bet you can use your super powers to read lots of words on your own, too."

ACTIVE ENGAGEMENT

Channel partners to find words they can read, keeping count across their fingers.

"Right now, will you and your partner work together to find and *read* as many words as you can? Look around the room and list all the words you can see. Count across your fingers how many words you can read. If you find more than ten, count across your toes too! Ready? Go!" I moved around the rug as children sat up on their knees, pointing and reading words around the room.

"I am hearing so many things that you can read! Francis reminded his partner that your names are *everywhere*! You can find them, and if you are close enough to them, point under them. Or just point to them. Either way, you actually *read* them! Karina reminded her partner that she can read all the class books that we wrote together! Remember, our books are here in the library." I held up the basket and picked up each copy, reading some of the titles aloud, such as "Things Our Class Likes to Do," "Things Our Class Likes to Eat," "Things Our Class Likes to Play." There are so many words and things to read in our classroom! They are all going to help us to grow as stronger readers!"

LINK

Invite children to use their pointer power to read the various materials in the tubs on their tables.

"I started a brand-new chart to help you remember this important reading power. Maybe we'll even add some more powers to the chart as you become stronger and stronger Super Readers." I unveiled our new anchor chart. "Let's read it together."

FIG. 1–2   Elijah points to a familiar word on a nearby vocabulary chart.

FIG. 1–3   Be sure to create an organized, accessible word wall in your classroom that grows with the children.

"Okay, Super Readers, are you ready to *activate* your pointer power to read *everything* you can? Remember to look at the word carefully, point under the word, and then *read* it. At each table you will find a special basket filled with all kinds of things you can read! Ready? Set?" I held up my pointer finger, as if releasing a powerful super power. "Pointer power, activate! Say it with me now, so I know you're ready."

The class chimed in, holding up their pointer fingers. "Pointer power, activate!" I motioned for them to head back to their tables to begin reading.

While most of your students will begin this unit reading from tubs full of familiar texts, you will want to be aware of any students reading conventionally. Provision these students with baggies of just-right books to read during private and partner reading time.

Rallying around the New Work of the Unit While Collecting Valuable Data

TODAY MARKS THE FIRST DAY in a new unit, so your conferring and small-group work today, as on any Day One of a new unit, will involve super quick table compliments, table conferences, and small groups, all done in an effort to rally kids into the energy and work of this new unit. Plan to move about the room as if you have roller skates on, stopping by at kids' workplaces to make sure, first, that children recognize the familiar poems, songs, and class books and therefore get into the swing of singing, chanting, and saying the words as they progress along, pointing to the words (albeit in some very approximate fashion).

Plan on seeing the kids making lots of approximations (i.e., mess ups). If the child points all wrong, with no one-to-one matching, you'll nevertheless celebrate. "Wow! You're working really hard to point to the words and read them one by one!" You can, of course, lift the level of the youngster's work, saying, "Can we read it together?" and then proceeding to do so with more one-to-one matching, but you can also feel okay about allowing approximations to stand because within the next few days, your minilessons will lift the level of the kids' work.

You will also want to take some time each day across this bend to help transition children to reading from book baggies of just-right books. Watch carefully to see how students are tackling the work from today's teaching and identify readers who demonstrate mastery of one-to-one correspondence and left-to-right directionality. You will want to take a running record to determine a reading level before providing these children with a book baggie of independent level texts. Set students up for success by giving them a book introduction to a few of these new books before putting them into their baggies. You might also add some familiar texts from your table tubs, an alphabet

---

MID-WORKSHOP TEACHING   **Rereading in Different Ways**

"Super Readers, eyes up here." I waited. "Super Readers don't just have super powers to help them point under and read the words. They also have super powers to *reread* those words *and* to do that in special ways. You can activate your reread power. Quick! Right now, choose something to read again."

The children sifted through their table tubs, retrieving a familiar text. "Okay, now decide *how* you'll read it this time." I pulled a poem out of a book tub to demonstrate. "Will you whisper read it?" I suggested, whisper reading the first two lines. "Will you reread with a beat or sing it?" I asked, while tapping my leg and singing a line out loud. "Or will you read in another kind of special voice? Thumbs up when you have a plan." I scanned the room for signals that the class was ready. "Ready? Set? Reread power, activate!" I added to the class chart.

ANCHOR CHART

We Are Super Readers!

- We have pointer power.
- **We have reread power.**

We have reread power.

chart, and a small copy of your word wall to the baggie. This combination of new and familiar texts provides an additional layer of support. Aim to have your whole class reading from book baggies by the beginning of Bend II.

In addition, make note of readers who are approximating the best they can, perhaps one-to-one matching inconsistently across pages, as well as children who will need much stronger scaffolds to attempt this work independently. While these students may read from the tubs of familiar texts a little longer, use this information to help you think about small groups you will want to work with in the next few sessions, and consider how you might need to adapt plans for the upcoming unit.

TRANSITION TO PARTNER TIME
Partners Remind Each Other to Use Their Powers

"Super Readers! It's time to read with your partner! Turn your chairs side-by-side and start picking things from your book tub to read with your partners! I know you know lots of things that you can do when you read with partners!" I pointed to the "Readers Read with a Partner" chart from Unit 1, which I had revised to support the transfer of skills into this new unit:

ANCHOR CHART

Readers Read with a Partner

- Put one book in the middle.
- See-saw read.
- Add a pinch of you. (I think. . .)
- Read the pictures and the words.

"Make sure you have what you're reading in the middle so you can both see and hold it. Then you can see-saw read. You can talk about your reading, adding a pinch of you *and* read the pictures and the words together. Remember to help your partner if he or she needs it! And now, starting today, you can remind your partner to use his or her powers—like pointer power or reread power—to be a super helpful partner. I'll add that to our "Readers Read with a Partner" chart. You ready to start doing that? Go!"

- Give reminders to use POWERS!

Give reminders to use POWERS!

Using Pointer Power to Read, and Reread Power to Read It Again!

Invite children to read and reread a Super Reader theme song with you, using their pointer power *and* their reread power.

"Super Readers, you are already using those super reading powers to read words *everywhere*. How many of you have read names?" I made a raised power fist to signal how the Super Reader could indicate *yes*. "How many of you have read labels on things?" The kids again signaled. "Here's another one: Has anyone read one of our charts?" They signaled. "Wow! A class book?" Again, the Super Readers rose to the occasion.

"Impressive. Let's use those powers one more time to read and reread this Super Reader theme song (a play on the Spider-Man theme song). It goes like this. Pointer power, activate."

> Super Reader, Super Reader
> Does whatever a reader can
> Sees a word, any size,
> Reads that word before your eyes
> Look out!
> Here comes the Super Reader!

"Will you all read along with me this time? Activate your pointer power! Logan, come up and point at the words as we all read together." I handed Logan the class pointer and led the class in a choral reading of the song.

"Did you see how Logan pointed under every word to help us *read* all of the words in this song? I wonder if you can all activate your *reread* power to sing this song now? What do you think, Super Readers? Okay! Say it with me. Reread power, activate! This time, Mia, will you be in charge of using your pointer power for the class?" I handed Mia the pointer and led the class in a rereading of the song.

FIG. 1–4 Singing is a great way to rally kids to the new work of a unit. Adapt song lyrics to popular tunes and use this as a shared reading opportunity.

Super Readers Use Pointer Power to Check Their Reading, Making Sure What They Say Matches What They See

MINILESSON

IN THIS SESSION, you'll teach children that the number of words they read should match the number of times they point.

CONNECTION

Direct children's attention to a prefabricated spider web bearing a note from Reader-Man, and ask a child in the class to retrieve it. Then read the note out loud.

"Readers, look! Check by the window. It looks like a *spider* web, doesn't it? Fernando, can you go over there? It looks like a note was left inside the web." Fernando inched toward the window, where I had stretched a thin piece of cotton, and carefully peeled away a small piece of paper. I unfolded it and began to read:

"Dear Super Readers,"

I looked at the class, "Oh, it's written to you!" I read on:

"My friend Spider-Man told me that you have been using reading super powers to read EVERYTHING around you. I have a MEGA IMPORTANT tip for you. Sometimes there are lots of words or longer words and you MUST check that you're reading those words correctly. I left you special power pointers, by the sink, to give you even stronger POINTER POWER! When you read, make sure you point one time, under each word to make your reading match the words on the page. Enjoy reading today and every day!

Readerly yours, Reader-Man"

GETTING READY

✔ Write the class a note from Reader-Man, explaining the importance of pointing accurately, and leave it near the meeting area. You may also want to stretch a piece of nylon or cotton to create a mock spider web on which to place the note (see Connection).

✔ Plant a pile of Popsicle sticks in a corner of your classroom. Children should have these pointers with them at their rug spots during every lesson (see Connection).

✔ Choose a familiar text. You'll use this as your demonstration text across most of this bend. We Suggest *Brown Bear, Brown Bear, What Do You See?* by Bill Martin Jr because it has a simple, rhythmic pattern that children can hold onto easily (see Teaching).

✔ Make student copies of a familiar text, such as a song, poem, or nursery rhyme. We chose "One, Two, Buckle My Shoe" (see Active Engagement).

✔ Hang the Private Reading/Partner Reading sign in an area visible to all students (see Transition to Partner Time).

✔ Choose one page from your demonstration text and cover the lines of print with a wide strip of colored paper. Write the words from the covered sentence on white paper and cut the words up into individual cards (see Share).

✔ Introduce the spaceman tool from writing workshop, and model how it can also be used during reading workshop. If you do not have this tool, create one by drawing an astronaut helmet and a face on a tongue depressor or bookmark (see Share).

✔ Add the strategy Post-it—"ECHO, Echo, echo read."—it to the "Readers Read with a Partner" chart (see Transition to Partner Time).

Debrief. Recap the contents of the note, sharing the new reading tip from Reader-Man and directing children to his gift to them: pointers.

I stared back at the class in total shock. "Wait, did I read that right?" I placed the note under the document camera. "Did Reader-Man just leave us a note about reading?!" The class stirred and looked at one another, and then Ori shouted out, "He did! He did!"

"Reader-Man said, that *you* have reading super powers! He left you power pointers by the sink. Sara, can you go check it out? Are there special pointers by the sink?"

"Yes!" she cheered, raising two arms up in the air. The class cheered and clapped right along with her.

"Well, Super Readers, Reader-Man just gave us a pretty important tip about reading words.

❖ **Name the teaching point.**

"Today I want to teach you that when you read, every word you say has to match a word you point to on the page. When you stop reading, there can't be any words left over or any extra words coming out of your mouth! If there's a problem, go back and reread, to make it match."

TEACHING

Read a familiar text, pointing under each word, making the pointing and the reading aloud match. Then name what you did.

"Let's reread, *Brown Bear, Brown Bear, What Do You See?* As we read, watch how I tap once for each word on the page. I am going to use my pointer power to make sure I point one time under each word and make it match. Ready to read with me? Here we go!" I held up an oversized version of the kids' special pointers and began to read aloud, as some of the children chimed in with me:

> *Brown Bear,*
>
> *Brown Bear,*
>
> *What do you see?*

"Did you see how we read that page? Did you see how crisp my pointing was? Was it on top of the word? No! Was it next to the word? No! Did I make it match? Yes! I read . . . one, two, three, four, five, six, seven, eight words! And I pointed eight times! One time for each word.

Feel free to make this pointing tool as simple or as fancy as you'd like. For example, you may choose to use plain Popsicle sticks. Kids will no doubt be excited, nonetheless. After all, Reader-Man left them! Or you'll maximize the excitement today's lesson is bound to create by embellishing these pointers with paint, stickers, glitter, and so on. You may even choose to supply children with little finger flashlights that they can strap onto their finger, lighting up each word as they point and read. For example, http://www.amazon.com/40-Super-Bright-Finger-Flashlights/dp/B0018LAGZY (link provided in the online resources). No matter the tool itself, your aim here is to make this reading work fun so that children are energized to practice. ✳

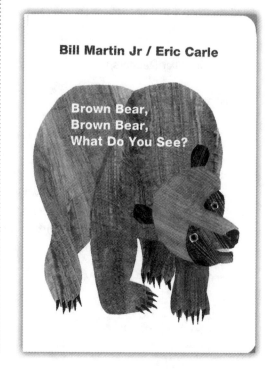

This time, deliberately omit a word so the pointing doesn't match, finding this out only at the end of the line. Use this to show the need to reread to make it match.

"Let's keep reading, and I will point again, using pointer power. Let's make sure I give each word one tap. If I don't, put a thumb on your knee." This time as I read, I deliberately made a mismatch.

> I see a [red] bird
>
> looking at me.

I furrowed my brow as I reread one more time, still omitting, "red" from the sentence and still coming to that moment when I finished reading and there were more words on the page. "'I see a bird looking at me.' Hmm, . . . I see some thumbs up. Did I make it match?" The class shook their heads, calling out, "Noooo!"

"Uh-oh! Reader-Man *did* say this can happen sometimes. So when you feel that 'uh-oh' feeling, try again! Let me read it again and make sure I point under every word, one at a time. I'm going to check for those finger spaces to move my pointer to the next word, one word at a time. Here I go:

> I see a red bird
>
> looking at me.

"Does it match now?" The class reassured me that it did.

Recruit a child to come forward. Give the child the pointer and recruit him to help you point under words, aiming for one-to-one matching.

"Let's make sure. Read it with me." I led the class in a rereading, pointing crisply under each word as we read aloud.

> I see a RED bird
>
> looking at me.

"Carl, come on up. Let's read the next part, and Carl is going to use his special pointer—from Reader-Man—and his pointer power! Let's see if he remembers to point *under* the words and make it *crisp* and *sharp* to make sure it matches. Here we go. Let's read!" I turned the page and signaled for the class to read the next two lines together. Then I celebrated the monitoring work kids were doing to reinforce one-to-one correspondence, matching written words to spoken words.

You'll want to make your pointing crisp in order for children to more easily identify the error. While many children will hear the error, having memorized the text you'll want to prompt children to study how your reading (and pointing) does not match the number of words on the page.

FIG. 2–1 Take the time to prepare a letter and pointers in order to create a drumroll for the work students will do across this first bend. It will definitely pay off!

Notice how I use a voice-over to narrate the behaviors I want all students to use, pointing under each word and making it crisp and sharp. For whatever skills you are teaching, narrating the positive behaviors, even before students are actually doing them, will help students put them into action more readily.

ACTIVE ENGAGEMENT

Invite children to read their copies of a familiar text, pointing and tapping once under each word with their pointer. Remind them to reread if the words they say don't match what's on the page.

"Let's all practice pointer power! Everyone take out your pointer and a copy of 'One, Two, Buckle My Shoe!'" I quickly passed out one for each child. "You all know this nursery rhyme *so* well. Get your pointers ready to read. As you read, make sure you point under the words. Tap each word once and make it crisp and sharp. But remember Reader-Man's *mega important* tip: sometimes you'll get an uh-oh feeling when the words don't match. If that happens," I paused to give the class a chance to fill in.

"Read it again!" a group of voices called back.

"Exactly. Make sure you match the words you say with the words you see on the page. Pointer power, activate!" I motioned for children to get started reading the nursery rhyme at their spot as I moved around the rug to coach.

You'll want to choose a short poem or nursery rhyme children know by heart in order to focus the work on monitoring one-to-one matching as they recite and point under the words. This way, students will be more likely to catch their errors when they have run out of words to point to or still have more words to go. Using familiar texts also will build confidence in your readers and will become supportive materials for them to read during reading workshop.

LINK

Remind children of the new reading power and pointing tool they now have, and of how these can help them read.

"Super Readers, today is so special because not only did we discover that Reader-Man visited our classroom, but he also taught us that readers have powers, too," I told the class excitedly. "Reading super powers! And he told us that one very important super power we all have is . . ."

"Pointer power!" called several eager voices.

"Exactly! You even have special pointers to make your pointer power even more powerful *and* to help you make sure your reading matches the words on the page. Pointing to words helps you not only look at the words but also make sure that you are reading what the book or song or chart wants you to!

"Thumbs up if you ready to go off and read! Are you ready to put your *pointer power* into action? Off you go!" I said, pointing to the Private Reading sign.

FIG. 2–2 A simple sign to cue readers that they should be reading independently.

FIG. 2–3 Gavin writes a thank-you note to Reader Man for the power pointers. "They are awesome!"

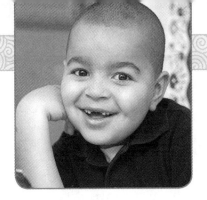

Supporting Children at Different Levels of Proficiency

TODAY, LIKE YESTERDAY, you'll do the work that is so important at the start of a unit. You'll move quickly among your students, giving table compliments and conducting table conferences and quick on-the-run small groups to try to hoist the whole class into doing the main work of this unit. Keep in mind that if you teach with power and if your units are well aligned to your children's development, your whole-class unit instruction should sweep up two-thirds of the members of your class, lifting all of them to new levels of work. You'll have given them tons of practice in pointing at words as they reread familiar texts, and now, with the added pizzazz that will come from them having special pointers, you should feel as if there is no one who hasn't been brought into the mainstream of the unit.

You will, on the other hand, quickly be able to see that your kids are at different levels of proficiency, and you will want to approach your instruction with a sense of if . . . then.

Some children may still need support with directionality. You might see some starting at the back of books they pick up to read. Coach these children to find the front of the book, locating the picture on the front and the title at the top, then move through the pages, one at a time, progressing from the front toward the back of the book. You might observe others pointing haphazardly across small copies of poems or charts rather than moving line by line, left to right. Prompt readers to put a finger at the top-left corner of the page, where the words start. Then, coach as they read across the first line, prompting them to return-sweep to the start of the next line. You might say, "Where will you read next? Move your finger to show me. Keep going!" To provide an additional scaffold, you may choose to leave a small sticker or draw a star at the place where the child will start reading.

Yet other children will have already secured early concepts about print, and they may be ready to read conventionally in just-right books. You'll notice that during writing time, these kids write with initial and final letters, and they can often reread bits of their own writing (you can as well!). You can conduct running records to learn the level of text difficulty in which these kids can be reading, making sure that you aren't expecting correctness (just one-to-one matching) at levels A and B. With these readers, your conferring will probably focus on print strategies that will help them read unfamiliar books and begin to move toward the next level of text, such as cross-checking the picture with the first letter of the word. Look ahead to the next book in this unit for the sorts of things you can teach these readers now in small groups.

MID-WORKSHOP TEACHING
Spaces between Words Signal New Words

"Readers, eyes on me," I said, and waited for their attention. "I want you to remember that you are not only readers, you are also writers. How many of you can remember writing a sentence like 'I love reading,' and after you write the first word—*I*—you leave a finger space before you write the next word—*love*."

I turned my back to the class and used gestures to show that after the first word (*I*), I'd leave a finger space before writing the second word (*love*) and the same for the third word (*reading*).

"Readers-writers, just like you use a finger space to *write* each word in a sentence, you can use a finger space to *read* each word in a sentence. After there's a space, it's a new word. The spaces can help you count how many words are on the page or on each line, and they can help you read. Right now, take whatever you were reading and, with your partner, count the words. Remember, after each finger space, there's a new word."

They did this, and then I said, "So get back to reading. And remember that finger spaces mean the same for readers and for writers: they signal a new word is coming."

"It's partner time!" I switched our sign to show the Partner Reading side. "Get your books ready to read. Get your poems and charts ready to read! Decide how you are going to read. You already know you can choose to read together, but you can also *echo* read. That means one partner reads a page and the other partner is the *ECHO, Echo, echo*, repeating the page." I added this to the "Readers Read with a Partner" chart to offer students another way to read together:

FIG. 2–4   Flip the class reading sign to signal that partner time has begun.

ANCHOR CHART

Readers Read with a Partner

- Put one book in the middle.
- See-saw read.
- Add a pinch of you. (I think . . .)
- Read the pictures and the words.
- Give reminders to use POWERS!
- **ECHO, Echo, echo read.**

ECHO, Echo, echo read.

I watched as partners settled in and made a pile of familiar texts to read, and waited to see if they picked up their pointers. "Remember, Super Readers, to remind each other to activate your pointer power and to use pointers. Help each other point under each word. Sometimes a reader will come to the end of reading and there will still be more words—or there won't be enough words—so you have that 'uh-oh' feeling. When that happens, partners, remind each other to reread."

Constructing a Sentence to Reinforce One-to-One Matching

Cover the words on a page of a familiar book with a strip of colored paper to reconstruct the sentence with students.

Once all the kids were settled on the rug, I sat down next to our *Brown Bear, Brown Bear* big book. I opened the book up to the page where I had covered the words with colored paper.

"Hey! The words are hidden," a few children called out.

"Yes," I answered. "The words are covered, but I bet you already know how this page goes, right? It goes, 'I see a blue horse looking at me.' I covered the words because sometimes it can be hard, when you are *reading*, to use your pointer power. It can be hard to make it match. But, sometimes when you are *writing*, it is easier to make it match."

Help kids transfer skills they have as writers to their work as readers.

I held up eight word cards from the sentence in the book and said, "These are the words from this page. We are going to invite a very special guest to reading workshop to help us get the words down." The class looked toward the classroom door, checking for an important visitor. I picked up a Popsicle stick on which I had drawn an astronaut helmet and a face, a tool the kids were familiar with using during writing workshop to remember to include spaces between their words. Looking at the little man, I said, "Welcome, Spaceman!"

The class giggled. "Hey, that's from writing workshop!" Jordan piped in.

"You're right! Spaceman came all the way from *writing* workshop to help us during *reading* workshop. How cool is that? Just like you use finger spaces to start a new word when you write, you can use the spaces in your book to notice when it is time to read a new word. Let's try it." I held the cut-up sentence strip in my lap. "How does this page go?"

"I see a blue horse looking at me," the class chimed back.

"Right, the first word we need is *I*." I taped the word to the strip of colored paper. "What comes next? Oh yes, *see*." I hastily stuck *see* right beside the first word, leaving no space. Then, I held up Spaceman and deepened my voice to interject, "Stop! This is a job for . . . Spaceman!

FIG. 2–5   Use a familiar writing tool to remind readers that spaces separate words.

"Where should this space go? Will someone come up and stick Spaceman in the right place so we know where one word stops and the next one starts?" I called up a child to insert the space to separate the two words.

"Now that we have that important space, let's reread and point, one time for each word." I pointed crisply under each word. "Let's keep going. What comes after *see?*"

"Another space!" Liliana piped up.

"Then, *a* comes after," Paola added.

I called the two girls up, one to hold up Spaceman and the other to tape up the next word. Before moving on, I invited the class to reread the first part of the sentence as I pointed under each word.

The class, Spaceman, and I worked together to construct the remainder of the sentence, rereading to point under each word crisply as we moved through the line. After we had constructed the entire sentence, I recapped. "So remember, just like you use spaces to write each word, you can use the spaces to move to the next word, pointing and reading one word at a time!"

FIG. 2–6 Spaces between words are often "invisible" in print. By placing word cards on top of a colored piece of paper, you're helping to emphasize the space between each word.

Readers Don't Let Longer Words Slow Them Down

Every Word Gets One Tap

MINILESSON

IN THIS SESSION, you'll teach children that both short and long words get one tap.

CONNECTION

Rally students to keep using one-to-one matching, even with longer, more complex words.

I sang the class gathering song and waited for the students to find their spots before I began. "Super Readers, your pointer power is getting stronger and stronger every day. But I have something to tell you." I leaned in, continuing in a grave tone, giving my words more weight. "Even Superman's super powers can sometimes lose strength. If he gets near kryptonite, his powers get weaker and he has to fight extra hard to power back up. And guess what? Some words (longer words) are like kryptonite for readers because they make it harder to use pointer power.

"Sometimes longer words trick us into pointing two or three times for just one word. Like look/ing or com/pu/ter. Words can be short, like *pen*, or long, like *computer*, but readers need to give one word one tap, no matter what."

❖ **Name the teaching point.**

"Today I want to remind you that when you point to words as you read, each word gets just one tap—even long words."

TEACHING

Invite children to say the names of three colored dots as you tap once under each one. Point out that even the longer (two-part) word gets just one tap.

I held up a piece of card stock with three colored dots across one line. "I have these three color dots. Each color dot gets one tap. Say it with me." I pointed under each word as the class "read" the name of each color:

Blue. Yellow. Green.

"Did you notice how even *yellow* got one tap? Yel/low is a kryptonite word. It has two parts but it still gets one tap, just like *blue* and *green*. There are only three colors, three words to say, three taps to give. Watch me one more time and notice how I hold my finger down to read *yellow*." I reread, emphasizing the work of holding my pointer finger under the yellow dot as I read both syllables.

Repeat this process with pictures of animals, again asking children to join you. Then ask kids to name which word was the longer kryptonite word.

"Now, here are three pictures of animals we know." I held up another piece of card stock, this one with three animal photographs ordered in a line. "Let's say and tap each one, one time.

Bear. Fish. Tiger.

"Three pictures. We said three words and pointed three times, one tap for each word. Which word was longer that time? Which word tried to weaken our pointer power?" Some kids shouted out, "Tiger," right away, while others murmured, "Bear," or "Fish," uncertain about the number of beats per word. "Watch me one more time, and this time listen for the kryptonite word that has more parts." I reread, pointing crisply and holding for both syllables in *tiger*. "Did you hear it that time? Which word is longer? Which word had more parts?" This time voices piped up with greater confidence, shouting back, "Tiger." "Yes, but even though ti/ger has two parts, it still gets just one tap."

Ask children to name how many taps—words—they will say for the four items you've placed on a shelf. Then invite them to do this work.

"Here are some objects I found in our room." I placed the four items in front of me. How many taps will we need? How many words will we say?"

"Four!" the kids answered.

"Okay, let's try it. Pointers up! Point with me." As the class read, "Eraser," aloud, I bounced my pointer across the first three objects, landing on the pencil.

"Uh-oh. I think the kryptonite word got me that time. This isn't the eraser! This is the pencil. Eraser has a lot of parts, but it still gets one tap. Ready to power back up? Let's try it again."

Eraser. Book. Pencil. Glue.

FIG. 3–1   Choose a variety of objects to place in a line for children to point at and "read."

Exaggerate your movements, demonstrating crisp pointing with just one finger. You will no doubt have some sloppy pointers in your class, who slide their fingers from word to word, cover a word as they point, or use a few fingers at a time. Demonstration is a powerful form of instruction, and you'll want to take every opportunity to model this work clearly for students.

FIG. 3–2   A reader points to color dots as he reads from left to right.

"Now let's read the words the same way we pointed to read each object." I stuck four Post-its on the easel. On each I had written the word for one object. "Pointer power activated?" The kids held their pointers up. "Pointer power ready, set, read."

Eraser. Book. Pencil. Glue.

"Phew! That was an extra challenge. There were some sneaky, longer words that had more parts, like pen/cil." I clapped once for each beat. "And e/ras/er." I clapped again, signifying the parts. "But no matter what, each word gets . . ."

"One tap!" the class filled in.

Be sure to choose objects that include both short and long names. Notice that we began this "sentence" with the word eraser to add the extra challenge of starting with a multi-syllabic word. You will want to see if students give this word one tap, multiple taps, or if they tap three words while saying this one. This type of activity reinforces the concept of one-to one matching.

ACTIVE ENGAGEMENT

Liken the work the class just did with pictures and objects to the work readers do with words. Give each partnership a copy of a familiar song to practice pointing to each word as they sing.

"I'm going to give each of you a copy of a song everyone in this class knows really well, because we sing it together all the time—'The Clean Up Song!'" I quickly passed around a copy to each pair.

Immediately, voices formed a chorus as the class sang the lyrics in unison.

"You know the words of this song very well, so right now I want you to power up your pointer fingers and make your singing match the words you see—giving each word one tap." I signaled partners to get started before moving around the rug to assess and coach.

I chose a text that I knew children would have no difficulty reciting, giving readers more time to focus on the work of matching spoken word to written word. I also chose a song that featured a few multisyllabic words and a melody that coached readers to hold their finger under longer words as they sang.

LINK

Compliment children's pointer power and remind them of the work they've done today.

"Wow, Super Readers, your pointer power is pretty powerful! Even those longer kryptonite words don't stop you! You power up your pointers and remember to give every word just one tap, holding your finger or your pointer down when words have more parts like eve/ry/bod/y and eve/ry/where. But remember, whenever you are reading and your words don't match, power back up and try again!"

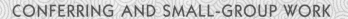

Supporting Students Who Are Below Benchmark

ALWAYS, ONCE A UNIT IS UP AND GOING, you'll want to think about the kids who are below benchmark and could use some extra support to be able to participate in the unit or to be able to continue their trajectory of growth. In this unit, many kids are not yet reading conventionally, so "below benchmark" refers to the fact that you may still have some children whose concepts of print knowledge are not firmly in place. You will almost certainly have many kids who are unsteady in their knowledge of one-to-one matching (which is the main work of this unit).

You'll want to plan small-group work targeted exactly to these readers. You may decide to help some of your kids develop their phonological awareness so they are able to segment sentences into words and to segment words into syllables. You could, for example, generate a few simple sentences that are meaningful to a small group of children: *Michael is wearing green and blue. Jennifer sits near me.* For each sentence, you could ask the children to make a tower (or train) of blocks showing how many words are in that sentence. The children could continue doing that without you—one could say something and the others could make a tower to match.

You might lead a small group targeted to the work of segmenting individual words so that children isolate and hear the component sounds. You could start with helping children hear syllables in the names on the class name chart. You and children can read out names and clap the parts of those names. You might say, "Super Readers, do you remember clapping out words to see how many parts they have? Each clap equals one part. You noticed that some words are short and have only one part (Sam) and some are long and have two or three or even four parts or more (Alexandra). Let's clap out some of our names to see how many parts they have. Let's read this name together: Charlotte. Let's clap that out. Char/lotte. How many parts does Charlotte's name have? That's right, two! *Charlotte* is *one* word, but it has *two* parts. Let's try another."

At this point in the year, it is important to identify and confer with students who are having trouble identifying the difference between a letter and a word. In a small group, build a known word such as a child's name or a known high-frequency word,

MID-WORKSHOP TEACHING
Matching Our Taps to the Number of Words

"Readers, here's a tip to help you make your pointing match the number of words on the page. You can count up the words before you start to read. That way you can plan how many taps you'll need on that page or on that line. Then, you can read to make it match."

TRANSITION TO PARTNER TIME
Partners Are Like Reading Teachers

I turned the sign from Private Reading to Partner Reading and said, "Super Readers, get your reading pointers and huddle up with your partner." I gave the children a moment to settle.

"You know how during choice time, some of you play teacher? You set up the stuffed animals and you take out a Big Book and actually *teach* them how to read! Well, I thought you could take turns today, during partner time, being teachers. You can do this by using your pointer while your partner reads like I do in shared reading!

"Will one partner go first, and teach your partner how to read? Remember, have your partner read aloud with you as you move your pointer to point, just like we did when we read *Brown Bear, Brown Bear*. Then, you can switch! Go ahead, super teachers, read and teach!"

constructing it from left to right with magnetic letters. Slide the letters dramatically to the left and say, "When I make your name, James, I build it letter by letter." Make sure to slide a letter when you say, "letter by letter." This language should also be used when writing. "When I write the word *the*, I write it letter by letter."

You may, instead, rewrite a few sentences from a familiar shared reading, using large print with exaggerated spaces. Explicitly point from word to word and ask the child to find a known word within the text. Use words with more than one letter (*like*, *and*, *go*, *the*, and so on) rather than words like *I* and *a* to make the concept more concrete. You might cut up the sentence into separate words, as well as cut up a known word into letters and have the child put the sentence and the word back together. Be very clear and consistent with your language during these activities to support explicit understanding. Use brief prompts like "Show me one letter. Show me one word." to check on a child's understanding of this concept. Long explanations can inadvertently cause confusion.

Be sure to keep these groups fast and focused, linking this work back to the job they have when they point and read words.

Developing the Concept of Words

Invite children to help you point to the words of a familiar song, "capturing" its precut words in a pocket chart. Prompt them to tap just once for each word.

I asked the children to bring their pointers and to gather in the meeting area where I'd displayed an empty pocket chart. I held the precut words to "Rain, Rain, Go Away" in my hand.

"Super Readers, I am worried that it is going to rain tomorrow, and I definitely want outdoor recess. So I was thinking that maybe you could help with a special mission. If we could all sing 'Rain Rain, Go Away,' maybe it would actually go away, and we could have outdoor playtime. You game to try?"

The children were pleased as punch. "I have all of the words to 'Rain, Rain, Go Away' right here." I fanned out the words so the class could see them. "You think that if we put these words up on our chart, you could sing and point to each word? *And* do you think you can point just one time for each word, even when the word is long? Do you, Super Readers of K-103, accept this mission?"

"Yes!" all of the children yelled enthusiastically.

"Let's start singing and capturing some words!" As the children pointed their pointers in the air and sang word by word, I placed each card in the pocket chart, leaving clear spaces between each word.

When we had reached the end of the first line, I paused. "'Rain, rain, go away.' Wow, look at all the words you've captured so far. Even this last word, *away*, gets one tap. Let's reread and point again—one time for each word." I pointed under the words as the class sang along. "Okay, let's keep going. How does the next part go?"

"Come again another day!" several children sang back.

I added *come* to the pocket chart. Then, I paused as I held up the card, reading, "Again. Again." I clapped twice to indicate two beats. "Do we point two times? I hear two parts in the word *again*."

"No!" the class called back.

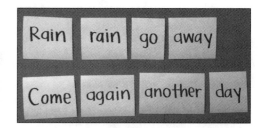

FIG. 3–3 As children recite the words of a familiar song or nursery rhyme, add the corresponding word card to a pocket chart or tape it to a piece of chart paper.

"You're right. One tap for one word, no matter what!"

I made sure to linger once again when we got to *another*. "Another. Let's all say that one together. 'A/noth/er.' Wowzer! That is one long word! Even though it has more parts, how many times do we tap?" All of the kids chimed back, "One!"

Reread the whole song as one child points to the words.

After all of the words were captured, we reread the song from the start, as one student used the class pointer to point under each word. "Super Readers, mission accomplished! You didn't let any of the long words trick you. Not even once! Your pointer power is *so* strong that when you read your own books, I know you'll remember to give every word one tap, even the long words!

Readers Use Snap Words to Anchor Their Pointer Power

IN THIS SESSION, you'll teach children that snap words—words they know in a snap—can help them fix their pointer power.

GETTING READY

✔ Have your word wall prominently displayed so all students can see the words (see Connection).

✔ You will need your demonstration text from the previous lesson. This text has a simple, rhythmic pattern and is either a Big Book or a text that can be placed under a document camera. We use *Brown Bear, Brown Bear, What Do You See?*, by Bill Martin Jr (see Teaching).

✔ Place a pile of pointers near your meeting area so that they are accessible to the children during your teaching. Children should bring their pointers to their rug spots for every lesson.

✔ Ask children to bring a copy of a class interactive writing book, such as "Things Our Class Likes to Play," from their table tubs to the meeting area (see Active Engagement).

✔ Provide copies of familiar texts such as *The Carrot Seed*, by Ruth Krause, in which you have placed colored dots under each word (see Conferring and Small-Group Work).

✔ Make sure the new strategy—"Hunt for snap words."—is nearby so you can add it to the "Readers Read with a Partner" chart (see Transition to Partner Time).

MINILESSON

CONNECTION

Ask children to bring a book from their table tub with them to the rug.

"Readers, before you take your spot on the rug, please choose a class book from the basket of books on your table. Bring it with you and place it in front of you. You'll be using this during today's lesson." I allowed an extra thirty seconds for children to follow this instruction.

Remind readers of all of the words they know in a snap! Rally them around snap words that they have learned and can recognize quickly.

"Super Readers, ever since the beginning of school, you have been finding and learning words that you can read in a *snap*. There are words that you can read in a snap all around the room—on our 'Class Name' chart, on the schedule, on labels and signs—and there are also words that you have been learning to read in a snap on our word wall. Everyone, point to the word wall."

The class turned their bodies, pointing at the nearby word wall. Look at *all* of the words that you've learned to read in a snap! Can you believe how many there are? Hold your pointers up high and use them to point at each word on the word wall and read those words in a snap. Ready? Go!" I used the class pointer to point under each word, moving randomly across the word wall, as children pointed their pointers to read each sight word aloud with me.

"Your snap words are getting even snappier! You can see and read *so* many words, just like that," and I snapped my fingers. "You're really lucky. Can I tell you why? You're lucky because the snap words you know from our word wall are *everywhere*. They're in your books and poems and on the class charts, too!"

Name the teaching point.

"Today I want to teach you another trick to make your pointer power even stronger. When you see a word that you know in a snap, it helps you keep track of the right words as you read, and they help you fix your pointer power."

TEACHING

"When I look at the words on charts and in books and in poems, it's almost like the word wall words light up and say, "Hey, I'm a snap word!" So, anytime I see those snap words, I can use them to check my reading."

Read a familiar text, pointing under each word and pausing on snap words to make sure your pointer is under the right word.

"Super Readers, let's read one of our favorites, *Brown Bear, Brown Bear*. When I read a word I know in a snap, watch how I make sure my pointer is right under that snap word. I am going to make my pointer power even stronger by making sure the word I read matches where I'm pointing. Pointers up, readers!"

I began reading and using my Popsicle stick to point under each word. The class chimed in, bouncing along with their own pointers. "Brown Bear, Brown Bear, What do you . . ." I froze with my pointer under the word *you*. "Readers, I need to freeze here for a moment because I know the word *you* in a snap! Let me check my pointer. Yes! I did it! I'm pointing right under the word *you*. My pointer power must be getting stronger! Let's keep going." I read the next word. "'See.' Another snap word! And look, my pointer is right under it. These snap words are really helping me check my pointing."

Read on, this time mismatching spoken words with written words.

I moved to the next page, moving my pointer less crisply as I read aloud. "I see— Wait! I just read *see*. But, uh-oh! Look. My pointer is under the word *a*. *See* is over here." I moved my Popsicle stick to point under the correct word. "Hmm, . . . let me try that again and make sure that I'm pointing under the word *see* when I read that word."

I reread, this time pointing crisply. "'I see—.' Readers, look with me. Is my pointer under the word *see* this time? It is? Phew. That was a close one. I'm glad I checked my pointing to make it match." I read to the end of the page, pausing at other snap words we knew and making sure my pointer was aligned to each snap word I read.

FIG. 4–1   A partnership points and reads the pages of a class interactive writing book.

At this point in the year, you probably have about ten high-frequency words on your word wall, in addition to class names. You will want to teach, practice, and show students how to use these words, not just during word study and writing workshop, but also during reading workshop. This lesson helps to show students how to read these words in a snap and how to use them as anchor words; that is, when they are pointing to one of these word wall words, that they are actually saying the correct word.

ACTIVE ENGAGEMENT

Invite children to read their copies of a familiar text, such as a copy of a class book, making sure their pointer is under the snap words they read—and to reread the text if it is not.

"Let's all practice making our pointer power stronger! Take out the class book you brought from your table tub and get your pointers ready. When you hear a snap word, remember to check that your pointer is right under it. If your pointer isn't under the snap word, will you just shrug and say, 'Oh well,' and keep going?"

The class chimed in, "*No* way!"

"'No way' is right! You should reread so that your pointer is under the snap word as you read it. All right, Super Readers, make your pointer power even stronger!" As the children began reading texts and pointing to each word, I coached in, noticing when kids were frozen under snap words and when others were rereading to make their pointer land under the snap words that they read.

LINK

Reiterate for children the new pointer power they now have.

"Readers, today you started to make your pointer power even stronger! I didn't even know that was possible, but it is! Every time you read a snap word and pointed to it at the same time, your pointer power grew and grew. Hold your pointers high and flex your pointer power muscles.

"You now can use your pointer in another way to keep building those pointer power muscles. Pointing to snap words as your read them helps you make sure that you are reading the snap words that are right on the page.

"But that's not the *only* thing you know about powering up your pointer power! You also know that you can count the words before you read to get ready to make it match *and* use the spaces to remember to move your pointer under a new word *and* to remember that every word gets just one tap, even longer words.

"Who is ready to work out their pointer power muscles? Off you go, Super Readers!"

FIG. 4–2 A reader highlights the words she knows to help her match her pointing as she recites a familiar poem aloud.

Using Small-Group Shared Reading to Support One-to-One Matching

YOU WILL WANT TO MAKE SURE that your small-group instruction reinforces both the work already addressed and the upcoming work. If you notice a few of your below-benchmark students are still having difficulty with one-to-one matching, you might decide to pull a small group to further this work. Say to them, "Readers, we have been reading this book, *Brown Bear, Brown Bear*." Show the students the Big Book. "I have put dots under each word to help us keep track of the words. Brian, your name starts with the same beginning sound as /br/own in *Brown Bear*. Why don't you use the pointer and go first?"

Note that you will have put dots under each word in the familiar text (or in part of it). Once the student's pointer lands on the big black dot under the first word, "Brown," invite the group to chime in as you read the book together. You might say, "Everyone read along with me. If you have trouble reading the words, that's okay! Be sure to keep your eyes on the word the pointer is under as we read." You can give each child a chance to do the work of pointing as the group reads in choral fashion.

MID-WORKSHOP TEACHING
Remembering to Point under Words, Not under Punctuation

"Super Readers, stop for just a minute. Your pointer power is getting stronger and stronger with every point! Can I show you something that can make pointer power a little tricky?" The kids nodded. I put *Brown Bear, Brown Bear* under the document camera and opened to a page. "Do you see this mark right here?" I pointed to the period. "What's this called? Can you remind me?"

"A period!" the class shouted back.

"Yes! And when you are using pointer power, remember this: readers don't point under the punctuation marks, like this period or this question mark. Readers only point under words."

TRANSITION TO PARTNER TIME
Readers Hunt for Snap Words

"It's almost time to read with partners." I held up the Partner Reading sign. "Here's something you can do together! You can go on a snap word expedition! You can hunt carefully through each book or poem or chart that you read, searching for *every* snap word you can find. Then, you can start at the beginning and read together, making sure your pointer is under those snap words when you get to them. What partners in this class accept this mission?" Children across the room raised their hands. "Mission accepted! Get going, word hunters!"

ANCHOR CHART

Readers Read with a Partner

- Put one book in the middle.
- Read the words.
- Add a pinch of you. (I think . . .)
- Give reminders to use POWERS!
- ECHO, Echo, echo read.
- **Hunt for snap words.**

Hunt for snap words.

End the lesson by reminding students that this new strategy can be used in other books. You might say, "Readers, I have made a copy of the words from *The Carrot Seed* to keep in your baggie. Notice that there are dots under the words just like in our Big Book, *Brown Bear, Brown Bear*. Remember, if you ever feel like you are having trouble keeping track of the words in the books and poems you're reading, power up your pointer power by practicing with one of these books. The dots will help you to point under each word as you read."

You might plan for two or three more opportunities to bring these readers together to practice one-to-one matching, making sure that over those subsequent meetings, you lighten the scaffold of the dots under the words. For example, readers could read duplicated copies of the same texts as those you have dotted, only this time, without the scaffold of the dots. You might give the students magic marker pens, and guide them to make their own small dots under each word, tucking in a reminder that a kryptonite word—a multisyllable word—only receives one dot.

You may gather the group together on another day, removing the scaffold completely and releasing them to greater independence. This time, encourage students to choose a familiar text from their baggie. You might say, "Readers, our pointer power is becoming very strong! The dots have helped us. But now, I don't think we need the dots anymore! Let's just *imagine* the dots under the words in our books." Support students as they begin reading their books privately, observing their ability to use one-to-one matching with greater consistency.

Readers Check that the First Letter of a Word Matches the Letter of the Word They Read

Teach children a new way to check their pointing.

"Readers, I'm so impressed by the way you're not just *using* your pointer power, but also how you're *checking* your pointing. I notice lots of readers making sure to read and point to one word at a time, so you don't read too many words or leave extra words behind. Point your pointer power in the sky if you're doing that Super Reader work on *every* page!" Children raised pointers up high.

"Do you think you're ready to learn *another* trick to check your pointer power? Here it is: you can check the first letter of the word you are pointing under to see if it matches the first letter of the word you read. So, if you read the word *balloon*, what letter should you see at the beginning?"

"*B*!" the kids shouted back.

"And if you read the word *turtle*, what letter will you see at the beginning of the word?"

"*T*!" the class responded.

"Right now, work with your partner to check that you're pointing under the words you know in a *snap* and *also* that you're pointing under words that match the first letter of the words you read. Go for it!"

FIG. 4–3   Often, the class name chart becomes a child's first alphabet chart. Encourage students to use the letters and sounds in names they know to identify letters and sounds in their books.

Partner Power Gives Readers Even Stronger Pointer Power

IN THIS SESSION, you'll teach partners to double their pointing power by having one partner read while the other partner points, and both check that one word gets one tap.

GETTING READY

✔ Choose a familiar text such as a song, poem, or nursery rhyme that children know by heart. We suggest "The Itsy Bitsy Spider." Place a copy of this text under the document camera or write it large on chart paper, and make individual copies to pass out to each child. You will use this text to support one-to-one matching (see Teaching).

✔ Bring table tubs to the meeting area for children to read from (see Link).

✔ Hang the Private Reading/Partner Reading sign in an area visible to all students (see Link).

✔ Make sure your "We Are Super Readers!" chart is accessible so you can refer to it, and take out the strategy Post-it—"We have partner power."—to add to the chart (see Link and Mid-Workshop Teaching).

✔ Make a small copy of your "Readers Read with a Partner" chart to use as a checklist (see Conferring and Small-Group Work).

MINILESSON

CONNECTION

Announce that *everyone* needs help sometimes—Batman and Robin, friends, even Super Readers—and that partners can offer each other help.

"Readers, I have something important to tell you. Here it is: we *all* need help. It's true! Doing things with help makes us even better. When Batman needs help defeating a villain, he calls on Robin to help!

"In this classroom, friends help each other in lots of ways! They help each other build with blocks, they help each other play games at recess, they help each other tie shoes. Think, what is one time a friend helped you just like Robin helps Batman? Turn and tell your partner one time a friend in this class has helped you."

There was a buzz in the room as kids shared stories of a friend helping them.

"Wow. It sounds like you all help each other every day! Guess what? Super Readers need help, too! Reading partners can help."

❧ **Name the teaching point.**

"Today I want to teach you that partners can help make your reading even stronger. You can work with a partner to practice pointing to words as you read them. One partner reads, and the other partner points to each word. Both of you can check that one word makes one point. This way you double your pointing power."

TEACHING

Invite the class to be your partner. Ask them to read aloud the words of a familiar text while you point under each word.

I projected the song "The Itsy Bitsy Spider" and said, "Readers, could you help me by being my reading partner?"

"Yes!" the kids called out.

"Let's take turns reading and pointing. How about you read first and I point?" I took out my pointer and pointed under the first word. "All right partners, start reading!"

As the kids read the first line, I followed along, making sure to tap one time under each word. "The itsy bitsy spider . . ."

Debrief. Name what you have done that you hope readers will do every time they read with partners, working on one-to-one matching.

Then I said, "Great job! Did you see how as you read each word, I tapped that word one time, even the long words like *spider*? Let's keep going, and remember, partners check as they go." As the kids read the next line, "Down came the rain . . ." I again tapped each word. When they read the word *the*, I stopped.

"Partners, I heard you read the snap word *the*. Let's check! Thumbs up if my pointer is under the word *the*."

Children gave me a unanimous thumbs up.

Make your pointing purposely not match the print to prompt children to reread and self-correct.

"We work so well together, just like Batman and Robin! Let's keep going." As the kids continued to read, I purposefully tapped twice for *spider*, so that my pointing would not match the print.

> *And washed the spider*

"Out? Uh-oh, reading partners! There are no more words left on this line for me to tap! What should we do? Should we just forget it and keep going?"

"No!" children protested.

"Well, what should we do?" I said.

"Go back!" "Try it again!" "We can reread!" Children called out suggestions.

FIG. 5–1 Elijah checks that his pointing matches the word he reads in a class shared poem.

"Smart. Let's reread and try it again." This time, I tapped once for each word, holding my pointer under *spider* to emphasize the word boundary. "Phew. That was a close one. Thank you for being the kind of partners that help me check, especially when things get tough." We finished the song, kids reading and me tapping.

ACTIVE ENGAGEMENT

Invite children to read copies of a familiar text with their partner. One partner reads and one points, checking to make sure that reading and pointing match, and rereading if it doesn't.

I quickly handed out copies of "The Itsy Bitsy Spider" to partners.

"Now you get to help each other! One partner read while the other points, tapping one time for each word and checking as you go. Remember, partners can work together to make their reading and pointing match. If it doesn't match, be sure to reread and try it again to make it match!

"Quick! Decide who's Batman and who's Robin. Batmans, you'll point. Robins, you'll read. Then, you can switch!"

I gave children a moment to choose roles and get started. I moved around the rug to coach them as they read together. When their reading and pointing did not match, I prompted partnerships to check this and reread.

LINK

Give partners a chance to continue practicing reading (and pointing) with each other before sending students off to read privately.

"Super Readers, today is a special day because today you get to double the strength of your pointer power by helping each other, just like Robin helps Batman! We might even call this partner power!

"Let's not even wait for partner reading time to practice this some more. Let's start partner reading time right now, right here on the rug. I've brought your table tubs for you to share. Choose something new to read and huddle up next to your partner." I gave students a chance to select a text from several tubs that I distributed in spots around the meeting area.

"Remember, when you read together, you can take turns. One partner *reads* the words one tap at a time, and the other partner *points*. Remember, Super Readers, if your pointing and reading don't match, reread to get stronger! Make it match!"

Children are far quicker to identify errors in someone else's work than when monitoring themselves. You'll channel partners to work together in this way, to support one another's ability to point and match spoken words with written words. As you coach and prompt students, make sure you don't just prompt the readers, but also the listeners to prompt each other. This way you are also teaching them how to work together during their partner time.

FIG. 5–2   Students can help one another monitor their pointing, making sure what they say matches what they see.

We have partner power.

I moved around the rug, coaching readers as they worked in partnerships. After a minute or so, I pointed to the Partner Reading sign and sent students back to their table spots to transition to independent reading.

Monitoring Partnerships to See If They Are Applying All They've Learned

TODAY YOU ARE FINISHING UP BEND I. This is a good time to look over your conferring notes and follow up on things that you have already taught. For example, you might return to a few children to reinforce the work of holding their finger in place to read multisyllabic words in their texts. You might coach readers to monitor their pointing, using the first letter of known sight words. Prompt readers to check when they are reading accurately, as well as when their pointing does not correspond with their reading.

Again, as you are closing out this bend, you will want to make sure that partnerships are applying everything they have learned about being a good partner—not just what they learned in today's minilesson. As students transition and get started on their partner reading, do a sweep across the room with your eyes and ears. Observe the partnerships in action and take note of which ones could benefit from coaching on things you have already taught. You might even use your "Readers Read with a Partner" chart as an observation checklist. Are they:

- Putting the book in the middle?
- Remembering to have one partner point to the words while the other reads the words?
- Both holding onto the book?
- Deciding *how* they will read the book (reading together or echo reading)?

MID-WORKSHOP TEACHING
Rereading Makes Readers Stronger

"Readers, I see pointer power in action everywhere I look! I know it's helping you become a stronger Super Reader every time you read. I want to remind you that you also have . . ."—I pointed to the second bullet on the chart—". . . reread power! Remember to read and *reread* everything you can. Rereading won't just help your pointer power get stronger, but it will also help your reading voices get smoother and help your brain do some big thinking work. And guess what? It can *also* help you get ready for partner time. You can reread to practice, and then show off your fancy reading work to your partner. Right now, find something to reread and put your reread power into action. Go!"

ANCHOR CHART

We Are Super Readers!

- We have pointer power.
- We have reread power.
- We have partner power.

TRANSITION TO PARTNER TIME
Taking Turns Pointing and Reading

"Super Readers, when you read with your partner today you can have more fun reading and pointing together. One partner can *point* to the words and the other partner can *read* the words. Then, you can switch to read the next thing, and then switch back to read the next thing after that! Make your partner power even stronger!"

Once you have observed for a few moments, you will want to walk around to a few partnerships, naming what you have noticed. You will especially want to compliment (notice and name) behaviors that a partnership might be exhibiting for the very first time. For example, up until now, a partnership may have been struggling to get on task quickly because they couldn't decide who was going to read first or how they were going to read. Today you notice that they got right to work. You might say, "Alex and Jory, I noticed that today you decided lickety-split that you were going to echo read! You didn't waste any time deciding. Super Readers do that! They don't want to waste a single minute of their precious partner time. Remember to do that every day during partner time." Noticing and naming emerging behaviors cements learning and helps ensure that kids will repeat this desired behavior.

After giving a few partner compliments, you will want to coach partnerships that still need work in one or more of the areas listed above. You may decide to work with just one partnership at a time, or you might pull together two partnerships that could benefit from the same coaching tips. For example, today's minilesson gave a new partner task—one partner reads and one partner points—so you will definitely want to support partners with this new skill.

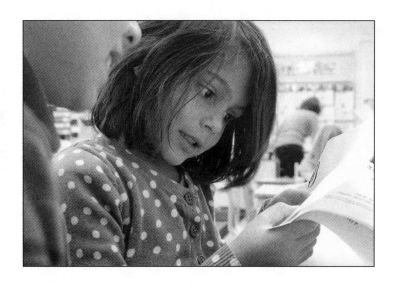

Choral Reading and Piggy-Back Pointing with Partners

Explain a new way readers can read (and point) with partners, spotlighting a partnership to demonstrate, before inviting the rest of the class to try it, too.

"Readers, I want to teach you a cool way you can read (and point!) with your partner. Instead of just *one* partner pointing, and *one* partner reading, you can *both* read and you can *both* point! You can read out loud together and put your finger down on the page while your partner puts a finger on top of your finger. You can piggy-back point to check that your reading matches the words you see on the page.

"Isaac and Josephine tried it during partner time today. Let's watch how they do it." I invited the pair to the front of the meeting area to demonstrate reading chorally and pointing together. I stopped the partnership to debrief. "Boys and girls, did you see how Isaac hopped his pointer finger right on top of Josephine's pointer finger and they read, tapping together?" The kids nodded. "Thumbs up if you want to give it a try! Take out your copy of "The Itsy Bitsy Spider" and go for it. Piggy-back point as you read together, making sure to make it match."

FIG. 5–3   Partners can read together to double their pointing power.

Super Readers Put Powers Together

IN THIS SESSION, you'll teach children to use pictures to help them predict and read unfamiliar words.

GETTING READY

✔ Make sure your "We Are Super Readers!" chart is accessible for you to refer to, and take out the strategy Post-it—"We have picture power."—to add to it (see Connection and Link).

✔ Select a demonstration text at level A to use in your teaching across this bend. We use *In the Garden*, by Annette Smith, Jenny Giles, and Beverley Randell (a Rigby PM Reader) (see Teaching).

✔ Mask an unfamiliar word on the first page of your demonstration text with a Post-it note. The children should be able to easily predict the hidden word using the picture. Use a larger Post-it note to cover the picture. We have covered the word *butterfly* and the picture of the butterfly on the first page (see Teaching).

✔ Get your "Partners Read with Partners" chart ready for use (see Transition to Partner Time).

✔ Ensure that all your children are reading texts from individual book baggies now, whether it be poems, nursery rhymes, word wall words, small copies of Big Books, co-constructed class books, or leveled books you have introduced (see Conferring and Small-Group Work).

MINILESSON

CONNECTION

Rally children to recall that every famous superhero tackles trouble with power.

"Super Readers, I've been studying lots of superheroes—like Spider-Man, Batman, Supergirl, Wonder Woman, even Reader-Man. And the thing I have found is that each one of them has *power*, yes; but also, each one of them runs into a ton of trouble.

"Right now, think about the superhero you know best, and signal when he or she is in your mind." They did this. "Now, the harder part. Will you think of one kind of trouble that your superhero encounters? Show me (with a muscle) when you've thought of that." They did this. "Now here is my question. When your superhero encounters trouble, does he or she say, 'Oh, dear me, that's too hard for me?' I better just go hide.' Or does your superhero tackle the trouble?"

The children all agreed that their superheroes tackle trouble with power.

❖ **Name the teaching point.**

"Today I want to teach you that when you are reading and you encounter trouble, that's the time when you *especially* need to activate your super powers. You can't let yourself get defeated! Instead, call on *more* powers. Keep using your pointing power, but *also* use picture power." I added this bullet to the chart.

We Are Super Readers!

- We have pointer power.
- We have reread power.
- We have partner power.
- **We have picture power.**

We have picture power.

TEACHING

Demonstrate using the picture on the page to predict an unknown word, then check the first letters and context to make sure your word looks right and makes sense.

"Let me show you what I mean." I put up page 3 of *In the Garden*, with a giant Post-it covering the picture and a smaller Post-it covering a word. "This book is called *In the Garden*. Will it be about things we find in the garden? Let's find out."

Look at the _____

"You might've gotten stuck on this word." I pointed to the smaller Post-it covering the word. "It's a long one! But this is not a time to *stop*! Don't let this word defeat you. Let's activate *picture power!*" I uncovered the picture and said, "Check the picture. What do you see?"

"A butterfly!" the children shouted.

I unpeeled the Post-it covering the word. "Now let's reread and see if that word makes sense here."

Look at the butterfly.

Look at the butterfly.

2

3

"Yep, *butterfly* makes sense. I also see the /b/ sound at the beginning," I added in, to support the work the class had been doing to notice the sound of the first letter. "Did you see how we checked the picture to help us defeat the trouble? That's how picture power can help us."

ACTIVE ENGAGEMENT

Recruit students to use the picture to predict an unknown word, and then guide them to use the first letter and context to make sure their word looks right and makes sense.

"Let's keep reading," I put up the next page with the picture and word covered. "Let's read together."

Look at the _____.

"Who's in trouble? I'm in trouble too. What should we do so we don't get defeated?"

"Picture power!" the kids called out.

"Check the picture!" others added.

"Okay, picture power, activate!" I took off the Post-it covering the picture. "Whisper to your partner what you think the word is."

Then I shared out some examples, "I heard kids say, 'Worm,' 'Caterpillar,' 'Snake.' No one said, 'Truck!' That's not even in the picture! Great picture power. Let's just check the first letter. Are you ready?" I peeled away the smaller Post-it covering the word, put my finger under the first letter and said, "*C*! So it must be *caterpillar*! Let's reread the whole page and make sure it makes sense."

LINK

Inspire children to go off and read by leading them in a choral reading of the "We Are Super Readers!" chart.

"Super Readers, you weren't defeated! You used your pointer power *and* picture power to help you read the words! When you go off today, I hope you don't run into *too* much trouble. But if you do, *don't worry*! You can always use your super powers to help you tackle it and figure out the words."

I pointed to the chart and said, "We Are Super Readers!" Let's read our chart together! Powers ready? Here we go!"

By masking the illustration along with the word, you're purposely creating difficulty for all your readers. As students begin to think about what they need to solve the word (such as the picture) then you can unmask the picture to help the reader think about what the word could be. This places more emphasis on searching for the meaning in the story and will help them read with more accuracy.

As your readers go off to read today, you will want to make sure they have all made the transition to reading from individual book baggies. For students who are not yet reading conventionally, you may fill their baggies with the contents of your table tubs (familiar texts such as poems, songs, shared reading texts, copies of co-constructed class books, word wall words, name charts, and an alphabet chart). As you work with small groups, introducing readers to new texts, these books can be added to the baggies.

Supporting Readers through Guided Reading

A T THE START OF ANY NEW BEND, you will need to spend a portion of your time rallying kids into the work of the bend, which means helping them accumulate more powers and use them together to read words with growing independence. We describe that work more in the write-up for the next session.

Although you will devote some of your time to supporting the work of the bend, the start of a second bend in a unit is also traditionally a time for you to lead guided

reading groups because the kids usually enter the new bend with baggies full of new books, and now, at this point in kindergarten, as children move toward conventional reading, this is certainly a prime time for guided reading.

Your guided reading sessions will generally be ten minutes in length, like most of the small-group work that you lead. You may bring a timer with you to remind yourself to stay within time constraints. Like all your small groups, the general plan will be that you talk with the kids for a minute or two, then they read as you circulate among them making lean coaching comments, and then you again talk to the group for a minute or two. Your guided reading groups will presumably involve four or six kids who read at the same level of text difficulty and who could use some support working with those instructional-level texts. Often this will be a group of kids who are just moving up into a new level.

You'll begin with a book introduction, which many believe is the most important part of a guided reading session. Think of your introductions as being designed to support the meaning, syntax, and phonics children will encounter when reading a book. One way you might start is to preview the text with the group. You might flip through a few starting pages and prompt kids to notice details and words. You'll also want to support meaning by giving children the gist of the story. Think about the story's pattern, perhaps saying something like "This book called . . . and on every page . . ." For example, you might say, "This is a book called *The Supermarket*, and on every page the dad puts something in the basket. What kinds of things do you think the dad puts in the basket? Let's peek at a few of the pages to find out." You might go so far as to say, "Listen to how this book talks. 'Dad puts oranges in the basket. Dad puts bananas in the basket.' Lots of books have a pattern like this one, in a list."

Finally, your introduction will presumably support word solving. Perhaps you'll call children's attention to a word or two (perhaps to *lettuce*) and help them solve those words, cross-checking the picture with the first letter of the word. Be careful not to preview too many words with your readers because you'll want to collect data by

MID-WORKSHOP TEACHING
Readers Try It Lots of Ways: Searching the Picture

"Readers, can I have your eyes up here?" I said as I stood near the document camera. "Some of you are running into some *extra* trouble when using picture power! Sometimes there are *many* things in the picture, and you aren't sure which one it is!"

I put the book *In the Garden* under the document camera and opened to page 12, where I had covered the word *snail* with a small Post-it. Pointing to each word I carefully read, "Look at the ____."

"Hmm, . . ." I said scratching my head. "When you check the picture it could be so many things. What should you do?" I shrugged my shoulders and gave a sigh of defeat. "Don't let even the picture defeat you! Try out a few different possibilities! It could be 'the snail' or 'the flower' or 'the grass.' All of those things are in the picture." I unveiled the word, and putting my finger under the first letter said, "Sssssnail! So, readers, don't get discouraged. When there are many things that it could be, try it lots of ways! Okay, back to your reading."

TRANSITION TO PARTNER TIME
Partners Help Each Other Check Their Powers

"It's partner time! As you are reading with your partner, remember, *both* of you can use picture power. Partners can help each other in two really important ways! One way your partner can help you is to *check* that you are reading the words on the page! As your partner reads, use picture power to *check* that your partner reads a word that makes sense. If they say, 'I see the bird,' check the picture to make sure there is a bird.

"*Another* way to help your partner, when they start to feel defeated, is to give them some picture power! Tap the picture. Point to the thing in the picture that might help. Remind them to use their powers!" I said, pointing to the bullet point on the partners chart. "Don't just say the word. Help them figure it out!"

ANCHOR CHART

Readers Read with a Partner

- Put one book in the middle.
- Read the words.
- Add a pinch of you. (I think . . .)
- Give reminders to use POWERS!
- ECHO, Echo, echo read.
- Hunt for snap words.

observing what students do when they encounter a tricky word. After all, learning happens where there is some struggle.

After the book introduction, children will read the book independently and you'll observe and coach, using lean prompts such as "Does that make sense?" "Use the pattern." "Try it again!" "Does the first letter match?" "Check the picture." When doing this coaching, move very quickly from child to child so that you can circle around to each reader more than once. As you gather data about students' reading behaviors, identify patterns of need. You'll want to hone in on one skill or strategy to elevate students' reading. For example, you may observe that students are using the picture but not the first letter of the word to read. Quickly demonstrate what that looks like in one place in the text and coach the children as they reread all (or a portion of) the text. Close your guided reading lesson by reiterating what you hope children learned. Children will add this instructional-level text to their book baggies to read across the week.

Readers Study Pictures to Make Predictions before They Read

Challenge children to use their special powers on each page before they read it.

To transition readers back to the meeting area, I sang the class gathering song. Children sang along as they found their spots around the rug. "Readers, we are going to do some shared reading of the book *In the Garden*. This way we can figure out what *else* is in the garden! Let's use our pointer power and picture power!

"Readers, another way to use our picture power is to use it *before* we get into trouble! We know that we can study pictures before we read the page, and that gets us ready for the words and what will happen in the book! Let's practice using picture power *before* we read the page and see if that helps us *avoid* trouble!" We read the entire book in this fashion. At the end of reading we talked about what happened in the book.

Then I said to the class, "Picture power is a great Super Power of yours, and it is helping you grow stronger as readers. Do you feel yourself getting to be really powerful readers? I hope so, because I do!"

FIG. 6–1   Two partners preview the page, using picture power before they read the words.

Super Readers Learn Words and Practice Reading Them in a "Snap!"

IN THIS SESSION, you'll teach children that readers look, read, spell, write, look, and read to make any word a snap word.

GETTING READY

✔ Make your "Class Name" chart accessible for you to refer to (see Connection).

✔ Prepare a one-day chart with the heading "Turn More Words into Snap Words!" and a numbered list of the steps for putting a word into long-term memory—"Look at the word. Read the word. Spell the word. Write the word. Look at the word. Read the word." (see Connection).

✔ Display the "We Are Super Readers!" chart on the easel and take out the new strategy Post-it—"We have snap word power."—to add to it (see Teaching).

✔ You will need the demonstration text from the previous lesson, which should be a Big Book or a text that you can place under the document camera. Make sure the text has pictures that provide clues to the words on the page (see Teaching). We use *In the Garden*, by Annette Smith, Jenny Giles, and Beverley Randell.

✔ Have some pieces of sentence strip paper ready for use (see Teaching and Active Engagement).

✔ You will need individual white boards and markers for each student (see Active Engagement).

✔ Place a roll of highlighting tape on each table (see Mid-Workshop Teaching).

✔ Ensure that children have alphabet charts and copies of your word wall words on small cards in their book baggies (see Transition to Partner Time and Share).

✔ Prepare a booklet of enlarged student writing paper and markers to use for interactive writing (see Share).

MINILESSON

CONNECTION

Celebrate reading progress by inviting children to read the name chart, and congratulate them for reading all the names in a snap.

"Super Readers, last night I kept thinking about the *power* you guys brought into this classroom yesterday. Picture power *and* pointer power. Can we just celebrate that power by doing some reading right here, right now? Let's read together, and will you read *loud* and *proud?*" I approached the "Class Name" chart and invited the class to read a name with me. After the class read one name, I gave my fingers a snap and said, "You read that in a snap, didn't you?" Then the class read the next name, and we snapped. This continued through the whole list of names.

❖ **Name the teaching point.**

"Today I want to teach you that Super Readers can make more snap words for themselves. If you want to turn a word into a snap word, you do this: look, read, spell, write, look, read."

TEACHING

Invite children to read two pages of the demonstration text with you, and be on the lookout for a word the class uses a lot. Then, work as a class to look, read, spell, write, look, read.

I placed the book *In the Garden* under the document camera and turned to page 4. "Let's read these two pages together and see if we find a word that we use a lot."

> *Look at the caterpillar.*
>
> *Look at the spider.*

Then I said, "Did you find a word that we use a lot?" The children suggested *at*. I wrote it on a piece of sentence strip and put it on the easel. "Let's turn *at* into a snap word. So we need to look, read, spell, look, write, read. Let's first look." I slid my finger under the word. "Is it a short word or a long word?"

"It's short," one voice called back.

"You're right. It's the same length as other snap words we know, like *to* and *me*. There are two letters in *at*. Okay, so we looked really carefully. Let's read it: 'At!'" The class joined me. "Now let's spell it: *a-t!* Look again. Do you see both letters? The letter that starts the word?" I pointed to the *a*. "And the shape of the word? It starts with a short letter, *a*, and the second letter is tall, *t*.

"Now, let me see if I can cover it up and write it." I held one hand over the word as I wrote it on the easel. "Does it match?" I asked the class to check my spelling, lifting my hand from the covered word.

This word work not only helps children build their high-frequency word vocabulary, but also supports transfer into context, helping readers directly link these words to the ones they find in their books.

FIG. 7–1   A teacher-created process chart to support building students' high-frequency word vocabulary

Session 7: Super Readers Learn Words and Practice Reading Them in a "Snap!"

45

"Okay, now let's read it once more: 'At.' Wow! You read that just like *that*." I snapped my fingers. "Tuck it in your pocket so you have that word with you forever."

"The really cool thing is that you can make your snap word power really strong by learning new words! This will help you read and, especially, to read with extra pointer power. Let me add this power to the chart, too!" I added another Post-it to the chart. "Let's read the whole chart together."

ANCHOR CHART

We Are Super Readers!

- We have pointer power.
- We have reread power.
- We have partner power.
- We have picture power.
- **We have snap word power.**

I can read I the book.
We have snap word power.

ACTIVE ENGAGEMENT

Encourage children to suggest new snap words from your demonstration text.

"Let's turn some more words into snap words!" I turned back to *In the Garden*. "Listen again for some more words that we can pull right out of the book and tuck into our pockets." I reread the first two pages as children raised their hands with suggestions.

"Will you turn and tell your partner one of the words you think you might want to make into a snap word for yourself?" I prompted the class to turn and talk.

Explain the steps readers take to make themselves new high-frequency words (snap words), and then demonstrate using a word from the demonstration text.

After a moment, I called the children back. "I heard many of you suggest the word *look*. Let's pull that word out of this book and examine it carefully, before we read and spell it." I jotted the word on a piece of sentence strip and put it on the easel. "Let's look at it closely. What do you notice about this word? Is it long? Short? Does it have tall letters? Short letters? Any letters that hang? Use your x-ray vision to study it carefully. Turn and tell your partner what you notice about the word *look*.

Select the words you use for this activity carefully. Remember, a snap, or high-frequency, word is a word we see in print so often that we want kids to read with automaticity. The first high-frequency words that you'll spotlight in kindergarten will be those on list A of our high-frequency assessment.

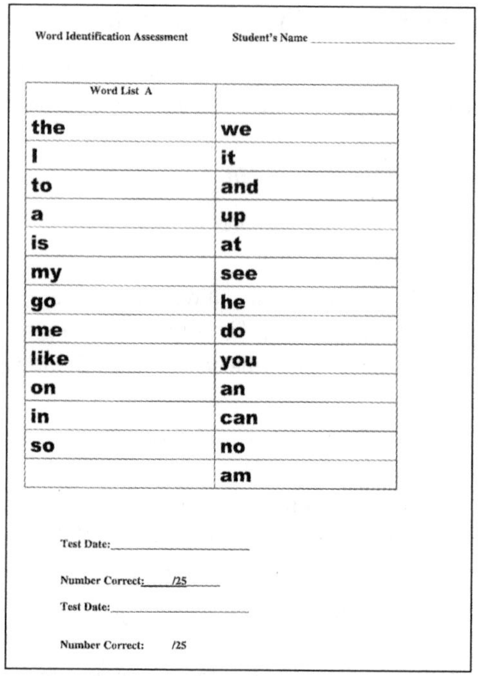

Word Identification Assessment		Student's Name _____

Word List A		
the		we
I		it
to		and
a		up
is		at
my		see
go		he
me		do
like		you
on		an
in		can
so		no
		am

Test Date: _____

Number Correct: ____ /25

Test Date: _____

Number Correct: ____ /25

FIG. 7–2 You'll want to use a word identification assessment to monitor students' recognition of sight words. By the end of kindergarten, students are typically able to read at least 25 high-frequency words.

"Okay now, readers, let's do what we do best. Point at it and *read* it!"

The class read the word in unison. "Look!"

"Spell it!"

"*L-o-o-k*."

"Will you study it once more and almost take a picture of it in your brain?" I motioned with my hands as if I was holding a camera and taking a picture. "Click! Got the picture? Close your eyes. Can you see it?" The children nodded.

"I wonder, if I cover this word up, whether you can spell it," I held my hand over the word. "Use your white boards to write the word *look*."

After a moment, I lifted my hand to reveal the word. "Now check it and fix it up if you need to." I gave the class a moment to do so. "Now erase it and write it one more time. Go!" After another moment, I asked the kids to check their spelling once again.

"Whoa! This class has some super snap word strength. Let's all read it in a snap. Ready? Go!"

"Look!"

Encourage kids to carry their knowledge of the new high-frequency word with them always, using that word often. Add it to the class word wall.

"Now tuck that word in your pocket, too. I bet that word will help you read lots of things!" I encouraged, acting as if I was sticking a word in my side pocket. "I'll add these two," I pointed to the cards on the easel, "to our class word wall, just in case you need to remember how they look and how to spell them when you write."

LINK

Prepare children for their reading by first reading all the words on the word wall.

"Before you go off to read, let's reread *all* the snap words on our word wall! I bet many of you will find these words in your songs, charts, and books as you read. I bet you will find other words that you want to learn by heart! When you read them, say them in a snap!" I led the class in a shared reading of the word wall, bouncing my pointer back and forth across the words.

"Everyone has these words in your book baggies. You can read your snap words before you read your books and poems and songs and charts today! You can study them by looking carefully at the shape and the size of the words or by chanting the letters to spell them. This will help you notice and read them in your books!"

By mimicking the act of taking a photograph of the word, you're nudging children to memorize the size, shape, and letters of the word. Over time, children should recognize and read these words with automaticity.

Find opportunities to visit your class word wall every day, if not multiple times a day. Invite the students to interact with the word wall in playful ways—joining you in a choral read, playing I Spy guessing games, reading the words out of order, and so on.

Supporting Readers in Building a Bank of High-Frequency Words

FOR THOSE STUDENTS who have mastered one-to-one matching, you might consider focusing on fluency. By now, most of your students can read each and every word in *Brown Bear, Brown Bear*, and our guess is that when you close your eyes at night, the words "Brown Bear, Brown Bear, what do you see . . ." repeat over and over again in your head! Before you say, "These kids can read this fluently. Let's move on to a new book!," stop yourself.

Reading—and rereading—*Brown Bear, Brown Bear* and other shared reading texts is helping build a bank of high-frequency words. Building a bank of high-frequency words takes readers one step closer to reading more fluently. Words like *what*, *do*, *you*, *see*, *at*, *me*, and *look* are words your students are going to see again and again in books, and readers will need to recognize these words with automaticity to concentrate their reading work on figuring out unfamiliar words. If they are able to automatically recognize these high-frequency words, they will also be able to focus more on the meaning of the text. To check for mastery of high-frequency words, you can ask yourself these questions:

- Can students point to these frequently used words in and out of context?

- If you cover up these words in the book, can they write the missing words?

- Are students transferring these words to their own writing?

Use some of your conferring time to pull a small group to do some isolated word work. Give each child a white board and practice reading, chanting the spelling, and recording the words. You might then have each child write the word on an index card to add to their book baggy, using these word wall words as a warm-up before moving into their just-right books. Help children transfer this word work into context, helping students hunt for these words in their books (and writing folders). Kids might even keep a tally every time they find a word. Teach kids to word hunt by pointing to the word, reading it, and spelling it aloud, then adding a tally to the corresponding index card.

If you notice that a group of students can read some high-frequency words out of context but are unable to read these words in context, you have great information that will help you plan for your next small-group lesson. Because words are often written

---

MID-WORKSHOP TEACHING   Hunting for Snap Words

"Super Readers, how many of you are finding and reading your snap words in your books, songs, and charts? At every table you are going to find some highlighting tape. As you read, if you find your snap words, will you put highlighting tape on them? In about three minutes, I am going to ask everyone to hold up where they found snap words.

"Hold up your text if you found snap words! Good word hunting! Now that you have found the words, go back and read the whole book! You will definitely read even snappier, now!"

TRANSITION TO PARTNER TIME
Practicing Snap Words with Partners

"Partners, after you have decided what to read, and *how* to read together, can I have your eyes up here on me?" I said, standing by the word wall. I waited for students to look up. "As you are reading with your partner, place your snap words in front of you. If you hear or see that your partner read a snap word, move the card under the word in your book and match it! The two of you can check it together, chant the letters, and say the word! This will help you remember the word and read it in a snap, always!"

differently in books, it may help to expose students to the same word in different fonts and ways of writing. For example, print several words in different ways—using capital letters, lowercase letters, and both Times New Roman and Comic Sans. Then have students sort the words and return back to reading these high-frequency words in context using familiar books like *Brown Bear, Brown Bear*. You might end your lesson by saying, "Readers, sometimes our snap words are camouflaged. They might look a bit different in books. That's no problem for a Super Reader! Remember, a snap word is still a snap word even if it is written with a capital letter or *all* capitals or using letters that look a little funny!"

The	and	go
Can	Go	THE
And	my	can

FIG. 7–3   Create word games to help students identify sight words in print, using various fonts and sizes.

Using Interactive Writing to Learn Snap Words Even Better

Rally children to practice new snap words by writing a superhero book together.

"Super Readers, will you please bring your book baggies and come to the rug?" I called. As students began to move toward the meeting area, we sang the gathering song together.

"Wow! Super Readers, you have been learning new snap words that you found in *so* many books and songs and charts! We have been practicing reading and writing them. I thought, to help us work on learning them even better, we could work on writing them to make *another* class book to read during reading time.

"Let's start by thinking about who we can write about. Hmm, . . . maybe it can go like this: 'Look at Superman fly. Look at Wonder Woman run.' How could the next page go? Turn and talk." After the class generated more sentences, we began our book. "On the first page we said that we would start with 'Look at Superman fly.' *Look* is a snap word right? Let's find *look* on the word wall. Shout out the letters. Take out your alphabet chart and tap it out. Sara, come up and write it. Everyone else, write it on the rug with your finger."

Call up children to practice recording high-frequency words with automaticity, and be sure to correct any mistakes on the spot so that your interactive writing is accurate and can be read easily.

"Everyone, let's check Sara's word with the word wall. Does it match? Yes! Great! Reread with me, and remember what the next word we need to write is. . . . Check the word wall. Shout out the letters. Tap out the letters on your alphabet chart. Carl, come on up to write *at*.

"Look at Ssss-uperrrrr-mmmmaaaannnn. Listen for the first sound in *Superman*. Show me on your alphabet chart the letter that goes sssssss." I wrote "Superman" in front of the children. "Reread with me, 'Look at Superman . . .'"

"Fly!" the class called back. I wrote the word quickly and we reread the sentence.

We continued, writing another page to practice identifying and recording sight words. The second page read, "Look at Wonder Woman jump and run," giving the class an opportunity to work on additional high-frequency words.

FIG. 7–4 Elicit simple sentences from students to co-create a patterned text.

Super Readers Make the First Sound in the Word to Help Them Read the Word

MINILESSON

IN THIS SESSION, you'll teach readers to look at the first letter and say the first sound to help them predict and read an unfamiliar word.

CONNECTION

Lead the class in a warm-up that reviews letter-sound correspondence.

I clipped the class alphabet chart to the easel as the children settled in their rug spots. Once they had gathered, I began, "Readers, you've been using this alphabet chart to point and read *and* to help you write words during writing workshop to make your stories easy to read. *And* I'm sure you already know that these letters can also help you read words. Let's do a warm-up. When I point to a letter, I want you to make the *sound* of that letter. Ready?" I pointed to several consonants randomly as the class responded with the sound of each letter. I moved to *g* and *c*, prompting the class to make both hard and soft sounds. Then, I pointed to vowels, prompting the short sounds of each.

"My goodness, this class is filled with alphabet experts! That's good news because Super Readers need to know all the sounds of the alphabet, especially when they get stuck."

❖ **Name the teaching point.**

"Today I want to teach you that sometimes picture power isn't powerful enough to tackle those really tough words. You can activate *sound* power, too," I added the new strategy Post-it to the chart, "using the sound of the first letter to help you read the word."

Add to the chart:

We have sound power.

TEACHING

Model how to use the first sound of a word to help you read a tricky word in the demonstration text when the picture isn't clear.

"Look at this page of *In the Garden*. I projected pages 8 and 9 so that children would see both the words and the picture. I had covered up the word *beetle* so that children would first rely on the picture to solve it.

> Look at the _____

"Hmm, . . ." I pointed to the picture and said, "I don't know about you, but I'm not sure what this is! What do you guys think?"

"Cockroach!" some kids called out.

"Waterbug!" others said.

"It might be a beetle," one child suggested.

"All good guesses," I said. "Looks like we can't just rely on picture power. We need to activate . . ."

"Sound power!" the kids chorused.

"That's right." I uncovered the word *beetle*, pointed to the first letter of the word, and said, "What letter do you see at the beginning of this word?"

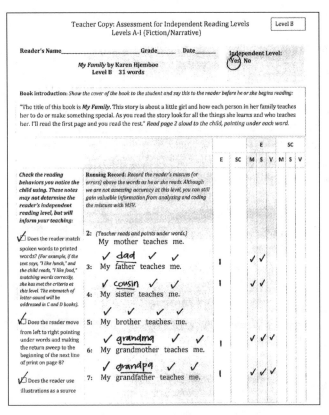

FIG. 8–1 This running record reveals that the reader is consistently using meaning to read new words and is ready for instruction that will teach her to cross-check with visual information, namely the first letter of the word.

"*B!*" the kids answered.

"So let's look at the alphabet chart to remind ourselves what sound the letter *b* makes." I pointed to the *b* and then to the picture of a ball.

"/B/!" kids called out.

"Yes. Let's say that a few times. /B/ /B/ /B/," I said, gesturing for kids to join in.

I pointed to the picture of the beetle and said, "So this funny looking creature must be a . . . beetle!"

ACTIVE ENGAGEMENT

Set children up to practice this same work on another page in the demonstration text.

"Good job activating sound power, Super Readers. Let's try this again, with another word. Hmm, . . ."

I pulled a book from the level C basket in the class library and flipped to a page with a word I knew kids would have trouble reading using picture power alone. I projected it so they could see and then guided them through the same steps we'd followed to decipher the word *beetle*, again directing them to make a few guesses first, then to look at the alphabet chart, say the sound of the first letter in the tricky word, and then use that sound decipher the word.

LINK

Reiterate that children can activate sound power to strengthen their reading, and remind them of the other strategies they've learned to use to read well.

"So remember, when you put your powers together, you can make your reading even stronger. Whenever you get stuck and the picture just isn't helping enough, you can activate . . ." I pointed to the chart as the class filled in "sound power!"

"*And* don't forget, you also have other powers. Let's reread the chart together to power up for reading today!" I moved through each strategy on the chart as the class read aloud.

I sent the children off by the first sound of their names. "Super Readers whose names start with /b/, off you go! Super Readers whose names start with /k/, off you go!" I continued until the rest of the class had transitioned to private reading.

It is important to demonstrate using the sound of the first letter, along with the picture, to read the word. Also, notice how I refer to a classroom tool, the alphabet chart. You will want to be sure that when your students are in need or stuck, they know that they can always refer back to some sort of tool to "unstick" themselves.

Supporting Students with a Variety of Small Groups

YOU'LL WANT TO CONTINUE working with guided reading groups today, building on the work you began on the first day of this bend. Carefully consider the needs of the children and focus your book introduction on the areas that children in the group need the most support with. For example, you may focus more on meaning and less on visual information if this group is struggling with comprehension. You might say, "Readers, this book is about a girl who . . ." and then look through a few pages in the text, deliberately using some of the language of the text in a conversational manner, so that students can then draw on this information when reading independently. Don't give away the story, but do pique children's interest, giving them a purpose to read the text.

As students read independently, circulate among them, coaching into their problem solving with prompts such as "Does that look right?" and "Reread and think about what would make sense." While you want students to have some opportunities to problem solve, you certainly won't want them to struggle too much. Overall, your aim is to have students read the text successfully. If you need to give a child a word, consider using the prompt "Could it be_____?" This offers support, but still nudges the child to initiate some action, confirming whether or not the word could be right. Occasionally following up with the prompt, "How do you know?" helps the reader identify a strategy he could use the next time there is difficulty.

MID-WORKSHOP TEACHING
The Alphabet Chart Can Remind You of Letter Sounds

"Readers, eyes up here a second. I've been noticing that for many of you, the same thing is getting in the way of your sound power. Sometimes, you forget the sound a letter makes! I want to remind you that when that happens, you can use our alphabet chart to help stir your memory.

"Charlie just came to this word in his book." I projected the page and pointed to the word *vest*.

"He recognized the first letter but couldn't remember what sound it makes. Let's help him!" I pointed to the letter *v* on the alphabet chart and then to the picture next to it and, gesturing for children to join me, said, "*V*. Volcano! /v /v/ volcano.

"So the letter *v* makes the /v/ sound." I pointed to the picture in Sam's book of a boy in a vest, and then to the word *vest* in the book and said, "This word must be . . ."

"Vest!" the children called out, Sam loudest of all.

"Don't forget, you can use your alphabet chart or even the name chart, if you need help remembering a sound! Keep reading and using all your powers to read words!"

TRANSITION TO PARTNER TIME
Playing Partner "I Spy" to Strengthen Sound Power

"Readers, it's time to meet with your partner! I thought one of the things we can do, after we read a book, is to play a fun, fun game! You can play a fun version of the game 'I Spy.' One of you can find an object in a picture in your book and then say, 'I spy something that starts with /d/,' or 'I spy something that starts with /k/,' and then the other person can guess. Make sure you each get a couple turns both spying and guessing.

"When you are done with one book, don't forget, read another book with your partner. *After* you read, though, you can play 'I Spy' with that book, too! Go ahead, start reading!"

After reading, hold a short discussion focused on comprehension, helping kids put together what happened in the book. Then end the group by giving a quick, one-minute teaching point that focuses on an area of need. Give students a little demonstration of the strategy in the text and then say, "Let's reread one more time and try that in our books." Listen in and reinforce the strategy, ensuring that students are able to read these texts independently before having them add the books to their book baggies.

You may also want to gather a group of children who are struggling to decipher the sounds of letters in the words, to do some interactive writing using white boards and an alphabet chart. Pull out a piece of writing that you have created as a class and focus on labeling five words. For example, if your class recently went on a trip to a farm, you may have a picture with several objects on the page to label.

Say, "We have so many things in our pictures to label and remind ourselves what we saw at the farm. Let's read what we wrote. 'We went to the farm.' Now, here," I drew a line next to the barn, "we can write the label for this thing. This is a barn. Let's say it slowly and listen to just the first sound, /b/ /b/. Like *ball*! /b/ like *balloon*! Look at our alphabet chart. What letter is it? *B*! Write it on your white boards, and Karina, write it here. I will write the other letters. At the end of the word I hear /n/. Like *nest*!" Write the word correctly and demonstrate the last letter.

Repeat with the other words, and each time hand the pointer over to one of the students, to reread all the words on the page. You may repeat this group, for about ten minutes for three days in a row, to emphasize letter work and phonemic awareness.

The active engagement part of the minilesson is a good time for you to notice if students understand the concept being taught. If you notice that there are some students who have trouble using the first letter to problem solve a word, you could pull a small group to reinforce this work. You might say, "Readers, I pulled you all together to work on our sound power. Today I want to teach you that sometimes you need to use double power—two powers at once—to read words." Direct their attention to the class name chart. You can say, "As I read these names on this chart, I want you to watch me. Notice what two powers I am using at once." Point to the *A* on the first name on the chart, *Amy*. Exaggerate the shape of your mouth to make the long *a* sound, /a/. The group can then chime in and finish reading the name, "Amy!" Move to the next name and point to the *B*. Make the /b/ sound. The group can chime in and finish reading the name, "Brian!" You might want to read a few more names in this fashion before guiding students to practice this strategy by reading a book from their baggie. Make your way around to each student, coaching them in this work.

Finish up by saying, "Super Readers, remember, when you are reading, it can be useful to use pointer power and sound power together to read words! Use your pointer power to point to the first letter in a word and get your mouth ready to say the first sound. When you do that you have more reading power, and the more power you have, the better!"

Stretching Out Words to Isolate Sounds

Lead your class in creating a class book by segmenting and isolating sounds in words they hear.

"Super Readers, we are getting really good at using sound power! Let's keep working on it! Let's make a book together, and on each page we'll write something that we like to eat!" I pulled out some sentence strips and put the first one on the easel. It read,

Jory likes to eat _____.

"Let's start with . . ."

"Jory!" the class called out, reading her name from the sentence strip.

"Read this with me," I said, and the class joined in to read the sentence strip:

Jory likes to eat _____.

"Well, Jory?"

She called out, "Macaroni and cheese!"

"Yum! Macaroni! Me, too! Okay, everyone say *macaroni*." They did. "Now we need to write it. Stretch it out like you do in writing workshop. Say the first sound slowly, stretch it out: /mmmmmmmm/. Check your alphabet chart to find the letter that goes with the sound /m/. Put your finger on it! Hold up the chart with your finger on it, so I can see and check. Jory, come up and write the letter that sounds like /m/. Everyone else, take out your magic pen and write the letter with your finger on the carpet space in front of you. Now on your hand. And now in the air!

"Let's read it again, 'Jory likes to eat /mmmmm/ macaroni.' Everyone, say the whole word and let's hear *all* the sounds, /m/a/c/a/r/o/n/i/, macaroni! Great! Let's reread the whole sentence. 'Jory likes to eat macaroni!'

"Now, look who is going next in this book! Fernando! Wonderful! Let's read, 'Fernando likes to eat . . .'"

"Cookies!" I then repeated the process with this word and then three more sentences to follow.

> Jory likes to eat Macaroni.
>
> Fernando likes to eat Cookies.
>
> Lisa likes to eat pizza.

FIG. 8–2 Focus today's work on isolating and recording initial sounds, calling students up to write the beginning letter of a particular word.

Super Readers Don't Give Up!

MINILESSON

IN THIS SESSION, you'll teach children that readers try one thing and then another when they are stuck.

CONNECTION

Use a story about Superman's perseverance to motivate students to not give up when they're stuck.

"I was watching one of my favorite Superman movies last night. The ending of the movie always makes me so nervous because Superman faces some *big* trouble. First, he tries to use his x-ray vision to get through a rock wall, but," I leaned in and dropped my voice to a whisper, "it didn't work. I thought, for sure, he was doomed. But guess what?! He used *another* Super Power. He used his super strength to pick up the heavy boulders. And he saves the day! You see, super heroes don't give up! And neither do Super Readers."

❖ **Name the teaching point.**

"Today I want to teach you that when one power doesn't work, Super Readers use *another* one! Readers try one thing and then another to tackle the trouble!"

TEACHING

Recruit students to read a new text, and feign a sense of struggle when one power isn't enough. Then rally students to use *another* power to read the word.

"Let's try this together with *In the Garden*. This mission might be tough, but we have so many super powers we can activate!" I gestured to our chart.

GETTING READY

✔ You can read a book that is in your library to have your students practice this persistence work. We continue to use *In the Garden*, by Annette Smith, Jenny Giles, and Beverley Randell (see Teaching and Active Engagement).

✔ Mark a page with a picture that might be one of several things and cover it with a Post-it.

✔ Make your "We Are Super Readers!" chart accessible to refer to and have the strategy Post-it—"We have persistence power."—ready to add to the chart (see Mid-Workshop Teaching and Share).

✔ Have your "Readers Read with a Partner" chart out in sight (Transition to Partner Time).

Then I projected pages 10 and 11 of the book. All the words were shown, but I had covered the picture of the grasshopper.

"Here we go, Super Readers." I spoke through clenched teeth, as though I was bracing myself. "Okay, I see some snap words here! Activate pointer power *and* snap word power!"

We read as I pointed to each word on the page:

Look at the _____.

"This word is a tricky one. It's loooong!" I pointed under the word *grasshopper*. "But we can't give up! We know what we can do!" I gave an exaggerated look from our chart back to the children and began to peel away the Post-it that covered the picture.

"Activate picture power!" the children chanted with me.

I studied it with a confused expression. "Activate picture power!" I repeated, but then resumed my puzzlement.

"Maybe it's a cricket," Logan offered. "Or it could be a grasshopper," added Alexandra.

"Hmm, . . . Picture power alone is not working," I sighed. "But we can't give up! We are Super Readers, and when one power doesn't work, we try *another*!" Again, I turned to our chart, located an unused Super Power, and with my finger underneath it, peered back at the children. I squinted my eyes and nodded solemnly, to signal this as a make-or-break moment.

"Sound power!" we exclaimed together.

"Let's reread the words we know and when we get to the new word, let's make the beginning sound and think about what would make sense there."

"'Look at the . . .' I see a *g*. *G* makes the sound /g/." As soon as we read the first sound, several children shouted, "Oh, it's a grasshopper!"

"Grasshopper, yes! That makes sense! Let's reread it, using all of our powers!" I said, and we read the page together.

"Super Readers, we didn't give up when one power didn't work for us! We tried *another* one and defeated that word!" I cheered as the children patted each other on the back.

You'll want to choose a page that features a picture that requires cross-checking with visual information, prompting readers to check the first letter of the word. You'll notice that we chose a photograph of an insect that might be a few different things at first glance.

ACTIVE ENGAGEMENT

Remind children that they will often need to use two strategies to read a new word. Invite them to use both picture power and sound power to read an unfamiliar word.

"Now it's your turn." I turned to pages 14 and 15 and placed the book under the document camera. "Remember all of the super powers you have," I pointed to our chart, "and if one doesn't work, try *another* one! With your partner, whisper read this page!" I removed the Post-its covering the picture and the words.

I listened in and coached children as they negotiated the print. When I called them back together, I named the reading work that they did.

"Super Readers, you pointed at the words with your partner, and read some of them in a snap! When you got stuck, you didn't give up! I saw you activate picture power and sound power to figure out the words on the page! Let's reread the page together. Activate reread power!"

LINK

Remind children that they can try lots of different things to tackle trouble as they read.

"Super Readers, remember, always, that you have many super powers. If one doesn't work, you are not the kind of readers who give up. No way! When you get into some trouble, you work to defeat that trouble by trying *another* power! Now you have your forever mission. Off you go, Super Readers!"

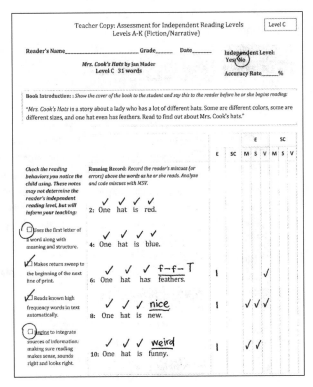

FIG. 9–1   If you have many children who are beginning to attend to the first letter to solve unknown words but not doing so consistently, you'll want to coach them to draw on all their super powers to read, using picture power and sound power do so with greater accuracy.

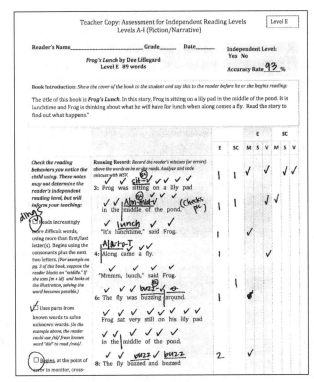

FIG. 9–2   For students who are already reading above benchmark, you'll want to consider the strategies they're using in order to coach these readers to integrate MSV and self-correct when something is not quite right.

Checking In with Individual Readers to Follow Up with Students' Goals

USE YOUR CONFERRING NOTES to follow up with students. You'll want to reflect on the teaching point you gave in your last conference with a reader. Use your research time to investigate progress. You might say, "Last time we worked on . . . Can you show me a place where you tried that today?" If there's no sign of progress, don't despair! Use today's conference to coach the child with this same skill, perhaps offering a different strategy to support this work. Don't feel as though each conference should address a brand-new skill. Instead, hold yourself accountable for following up, just as much as you hold the student accountable for practicing independently. Then, if further support is needed, offer additional strategies to accelerate progress. If, however, the student is progressing nicely with the skill, consider other next steps to address.

As you near the end of the bend, if you haven't done so already, be sure to lead a third guided reading session with any groups of children you've met with already during this bend. There are several ways you might structure these groups. The goal is to release even more scaffolds so that children begin to read new books with increasing independence, now doing the things you've modeled for them up until this point.

You could give a brief introduction, saying just one or two sentences about the text and then invite the children in the group to get ready to read the book, previewing it as they keep in mind what you've told them. Children might look for words that they know, study the pictures carefully, and think about what this book will be about.

As children read, you will want to begin by offering very light scaffolds such as nonverbal prompts, pointing to charts or strategy cards to remind them of things they've learned. First, try to see if students are able to initiate the strategy work without your voiceover. This way, you offer a very light scaffold, but the actual execution of the work is left to the kids themselves. If students are struggling, then resort to a heavy scaffold such as giving a lean direction.

After students have practiced in a few books and your ten minutes are winding down, you will want to point out that students were able to work with lots of independence. As a way to support their continued work, you might say to them, "I hardly had to do anything! All I did was point to the card or the picture in your book! I bet you could do that for yourselves too! Keep reading and reminding *yourselves* what things you can do to help you read better!"

MID-WORKSHOP TEACHING
Celebrating Persistence

"Readers, give me your eyes for a moment. I am noticing some really important things happening. I've been finding readers who are not just activating *one* Super Power when they get stuck, but two and three super powers! They are trying *another* and *another*! That is super *fearless* reading, and it is also called something else. It is called being persistent! Readers don't give up when things get tough. Being persistent is really something special. I think we need to make it a power, let's call it persistence power!" I added it to the chart.

- **We have persistence power.**

"Yeah!" the children responded.

"Readers, everyone, be persistent! When one power doesn't work, try another and another until you get it!" I raised my arm in the air, and with a clenched fist I exclaimed, "Persistence power!" which the children repeated, and then they returned to reading.

Partners Give Reminders When Their Partner Is Stuck

"Super Readers, it's time for partner reading! Before you start, I want to tell you something: partners can remind each other to have persistence power. Instead of telling a partner the word when she gets stuck, Super Readers can give that partner some time, and then, some reminders from our chart, like 'Try picture power,' or 'Try *another* power!'"

ANCHOR CHART

Readers Read with a Partner

- Put one book in the middle.
- See-saw read.
- Add a pinch of you. (I think . . .)
- Read the pictures and the words.
- Give reminders to use POWERS!
- ECHO, Echo, echo read.
- Hunt for snap words.

Using Persistence to Fix Up Words

Show readers that having persistence power helps when solving words and also when fixing up words.

As the children gathered back in the meeting area, I pointed to the new entry on our chart.

"I have something else important to tell you, readers. We know that persistence power can be used when you get stuck and have to figure out a hard word. But sometimes, readers think they've defeated a hard word and then realize that something is not quite right. When that happens, readers can use persistence power to fix it up! Did this happen for any of you as you read today? Thumbs up if you activated your persistence power!"

I saw David and Karina waving their thumbs in the air, and asked them to share their experience.

We have persistence power.

"We thought one mom was a police," Karina said. I interrupted her to say, "Hold up your book so we know what you're reading." She did and I said, "Oh, *Moms!* That's a great book. It tells about what jobs different moms do, right?"

"Yup," David said. "And we thought this mom was a police." He flipped to the page and pointed to the picture. "But then we realized it didn't match the words." He pointed to them.

"Yeah, so we used pointer power and realized there are *two* words here," Karina interjected.

"So then we used persistence power to fix it up," David said.

"And what do you think they tried next?" I asked the rest of the class. "Actually, why don't you try it yourselves?" I borrowed the book and placed it under the document camera. "Turn and talk to the person next to you. Use *another* Super Power to fix up this part!"

After I listened in and coached readers, I called them back together. "Wow, Super Readers. Some of you tried pointer power *and* reread power *and* picture power and realized that a word that could go there is *officer*, because you have heard of a *police officer* before. That matches! Some of you used picture power *and* sound power; you said /o/ when you looked at the beginning of the word and then the rest of the word just came right out! I saw that all of you tried more than one way to fix up this word. How persistent! Thumbs up if you activated persistence power today." Each child raised a thumb and left the meeting area knowing that trying and trying again is highly valued.

Session 10

Celebration
Readers Show Off Their Powers

MINILESSON

In the connection, you might lead children through a shared reading of the "We Are Super Readers!" anchor chart. Give this a celebratory feel. Point to the chart and say something like, "Holy moly, Super Readers, look at all the reading powers you know how to activate now! Let's read this list together in big Super Reader voices." You might invite a kid up to point to each power as the class reads the list together.

ANCHOR CHART

We Are Super Readers!

- We have pointer power.
- We have reread power.
- We have partner power.
- We have picture power.
- We have snap word power.
- We have sound power.
- We have persistence power.

Then, name the teaching point. Say, "Today I want to teach you that once readers are able to activate *lots* of powers, they make sure to check in on these, noticing which ones they use *all* the time and which ones they need to power up. Then they set goals."

During the teaching, model how you refer to the chart to notice which powers you use all the time (highlight two or three). Then pause and make the "realization" that you aren't using one or two powers enough. Say, "Uh-oh! I don't think I'm being persistent *all* the time. I need to power up my persistence power!" Then demonstrate how you go about setting a concrete goal to try to be persistent *every time* you read. Make a quick sketch of a capital *P* inside a star shape (or any icon that you'd like to use to represent persistence) on a Post-it and slap it on your baggie of books as a reminder to yourself to try harder and harder each time reading feels tough. Hold it up for children to see. Then quickly repeat this process for a second power so that children see you making not one, but two goals.

In the active engagement, channel partners to work together to identify the things they are doing *always* (or mostly) as they read and the things they need reminders to do. Suggest that they put goal Post-its on their own book baggies. You may want to encourage kids to create their own symbols to represent powers—maybe a finger for pointer power, two stick figures for partner power, and so on. You can also guide kids to use the icons on the class anchor chart. Encourage partners to hold each other accountable for coming up with more than one goal and then to quickly practice powering up that strategy with each other.

For the link, congratulate children for identifying and setting goals, and nudge them to keep these in mind as they read, and to affix their goal Post-it notes to their tables for now, as easy reminders. Point out, too, that they have a long list of powers they can activate as they read—not just the ones they are forgetting.

CONFERRING AND SMALL-GROUP WORK

As you confer and pull small groups today, use the "We Are Super Readers" anchor chart as a checklist to form your own assessments of your students' reading strategy use. What are kids doing with automaticity? Which skills will you need to revisit in the next bend? Use this time to set yourself up for future instruction.

In your mid-workshop teaching, teach children that rereading is a great way to put all of their reading powers together. Because they'll now be familiar with a book, they can put their energy into making sure they are activating *all* their powers, using them at the same time to be Super Readers.

As you transition to partner time, suggest that children practice their best moves with their partner—that they put their best moves together as they read. Partners might also use the chart as a checklist and take turns reading to each other. The listening partner can then use the chart to give reminders like, "Don't forget to activate sound power!"

Today's share session offers you the perfect chance to celebrate the work of this bend. Invite children to show off their powers! Ask them to think, "What is my very *best* move?" and "What *else* can I do?" Kids can work in small groups on the rug, practicing a book reading that shows off each of their strongest skills. Then each small group can perform a reading for the rest of the class. At the end, you might reward each child with a special cape that they can wear the rest of the day. Be sure to make this moment feel big. Say, "Class K, at the beginning of this unit, Reader-Man left each one of you a special pointer. Wave it in the air now!" Then say, "That feels like ages ago, doesn't it? Now you can do so much more than point! You can . . ." List each power off the chart and then say, "You have become *Super Readers*. You rank right up there with Spider-Man, Supergirl, Wonder Woman, and Reader-Man—with all of the super heroes! You have earned your capes!" Then you might either give each child a Super Reader cape you have constructed out of construction paper or fabric, or you could invite each child to make her own.

Readers Use Their Voices to Bring Books to Life

IN THIS SESSION, you'll teach children that readers read with smooth voices to bring books to life.

GETTING READY

✔ Make the "We Are Super Readers!" chart accessible (see Connection).

✔ Choose any familiar text, matching the level of most readers in the class, to demonstrate what it sounds like to read with fluency. In this case, we used *In the Garden*, by Annette Smith, Jenny Giles, and Beverley Randell (see Teaching and Active Engagement).

✔ Ask students to bring one book they know well from their reading baggie to read to a partner (see Link).

✔ Prepare a copy of "Rain, Rain, Go Away" written on chart paper, to practice reading with fluent voices (see Share).

MINILESSON

CONNECTION

Inform students that now that they have many reading powers, they have the responsibility to bring books to life.

With the class gathering song, I transitioned the students to the rug. We sat around our well-known and loved "We Are Super Readers!" chart. "Super Readers, you now have *many* super powers. That's *big* news!" I gestured toward the chart. "You don't have just one power or two. Let's count them, together. One, two, three, four, five, six, seven! Seven powers! Look at them all! Lets read them to make sure they are all activated." The students' eyes grew wide with pride as we began to read through each one of their powers.

I shifted my excited tone to one that was much more serious as I gave the next bit of news. "Super-heroes have many powers too, just like you, but with these powers comes great responsibility. Superheroes have the responsibility to use their powers to keep people safe, and you, Super Readers, have a great responsibility as well. You have the responsibility to bring books to life!"

❖ **Name the teaching point.**

"Today I want to teach you that when you use all your super powers, you can bring books to life. You can read them to others just as grown-ups read books to you, and you can read them to yourself that way as well."

TEACHING

Invite children to bring the familiar text to life with you, reading in smooth reading voices.

"Let's read *In the Garden*. We can't just read it like any old readers. We need to bring this book to life using our smoothest reading voices." I cleared my throat for dramatic effect. "Eh-eh-em. Get your voices ready, readers!" The class excitedly cleared their throats with me as we prepared for our smoothest reading voices for the hard work that was to come.

"Let's go! Read with me!" We read the first page of *In the Garden*. I read with a loud voice, modeling what a smooth reading voice should sound like so that the kids could mimic my expression.

"'Look at the butterfly.' Readers, did you hear how we brought that page to life? We were quite dramatic. We didn't read it in any old, choppy way. We used our smoothest voice to make this page pop almost right out of the book! Let's see if we can bring the next page to life as well."

I turned the page and continued on, inviting the children to join in.

"'Look at the caterpillar.' Our voices are so smooth and sound very dramatic, I can actually picture the caterpillar crawling around the garden. We really are bringing this book to life!"

Deliberately read in a choppy voice, going back to smooth it out.

"All right, readers, let's keep going in our smoothest voices." I read the next page with choppy expression, reading word by word. "'Look. At. The. Spider.'" A small commotion broke out.

"No!" shouted Liliana. "That was not smooth!"

"Oh no, you're right! That wasn't smooth at all. I sounded almost like a robot! Let's try it again. Help me to read in my smoothest voice and bring this page to life." We read the page again, and this time I led the class with a smooth and expressive voice. "'Look at the spider.' That was much better, and now I can actually *see* the spider spinning his web. I might even read this again to sound a little bit creepy and crawly like the spider." I reread, adding a bit more expression. We continued on, bringing the next few pages alive by reading in our smoothest reading voices.

"Thank you for helping me bring that book to life. When my voice started. To. Sound. Choppy. You helped me smoooooth it out! When you read, the same thing might happen. Don't worry. You can always go back and reread, making your voice smoother."

ANCHOR CHART

We Are Super Readers!

- We have pointer power.
- We have reread power.
- We have partner power.
- We have picture power.
- We have snap word power.
- We have sound power.
- We have persistence power.

Your emergent readers are working on one-to-one match as they read. Each time they reread their books (or poems or charts), you should see that their fluency improves. This is why we chose to work on fluency in a familiar book, rather than in a first read of a new text. Expect students to build fluency when they reread increasingly more familiar texts during reading workshop.

Notice how I invite students to read along with me. My voice is fluent, highly expressive, and louder than the rest. I invite students along during the demonstration to give them the opportunity to practice more. This will also keep your students actively thinking and thus more cognitively engaged during the lesson.

ACTIVE ENGAGEMENT

Children will finish reading the same familiar book, continuing to practice the work of bringing books to life using a smooth reading voice.

"Do you think you can use *all* your super powers to bring this book to life and read it to *me?* Remember to get your voices ready, to read with your smoothest reading voices. Eh-eh-eh-em." I turned the page, inviting the students to begin reading aloud in unison.

"Wow, readers! You are really bringing this book to life! Thumbs up if you can make the next page sound just as smooth." I was met with a sea of excited thumbs. "All right, let's hear it!"

The children read the next page, and then I asked them to reflect on their reading. "Readers, was that your smoothest voice? Did you really make that page come alive?"

"Yes!" They all called out in unison.

"All right, let's keep going!" We continued on to the end of the book, taking time to reflect and smooth out any pages that we didn't bring to life the first time around.

LINK

Give children another opportunity to practice bringing what they read to life with the texts they brought from their book baggies.

"Super Readers, with all those reading powers you have, you can bring everything you read to life! Don't let those books, poems, songs, or charts down by reading them in a boring or choppy way. Take out what you brought with you from your baggie. Turn in toward your reading partners and take turns reading to each other, making your voice sound just like mine when I read to you. Read with a smooth and dramatic voice. Ready? Go!"

The students began reading to one another as I quickly listened in and coached. After a minute or so, I went back to the front of the class and gained their attention. "Super Readers, it is clear that you are ready to take on this great responsibility of bringing your books to life, when you read to someone *and* when you read to yourself."

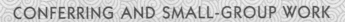
Coaching Readers to Develop Their Fluency

AT THE BEGINNING OF THIS NEW BEND, you will want to do two things. First, you will want to support the new work in this bend, helping readers bring their reading to life. You will want to help them find ways to read with more fluency, that is, with more expression in their voice and more prosody that maintains the syntax and meaning of the texts.

It is also important to keep in mind that students will not necessarily sound very fluent on the first reading of a book.

When you approach your students in a conference, be sure to ask them, "How many times have you read this book?" or "Is this the first time you have read this book?" You will want to encourage students to work on rereading their books. With each rereading, students should be able to say more about what their book is about, as well as read it with increasing fluency. You may decide to play the perfect partner in your conferences with readers and work on choral or echo reading with them to help students read with more fluency.

Don't forget to work with your more advanced readers, readers who may be reading conventionally and using letters and sounds to help them read. They, too, as they reread their books, will be working on fluency. But first, there is quite a bit of work they have to do for getting through a first reading in new books in their baggies. You may want to start a small group and coach them on using more letters and sounds as they read their books for the first time. Ask students to bring their book baggies and stack up three books that they haven't read yet. Say to readers, "I know that many of you have new books to read in your baggies and that there will be hard words that you need to tackle. Don't forget to look closely at the letters in the beginning of the word and say the sounds you see. Then ask yourself, 'What would make sense here?' Are you ready? Let's start reading our books."

MID-WORKSHOP TEACHING
Readers Activate Reread Power to Bring Books to Life

"Readers, can I stop you for a moment? I want to remind you that when you want to read your book aloud *really, really* well, so people pull in to listen and say 'Ahhhh,' at the end, it is important to read it smooooothly. Not. Like. A. Robot. And guess what? Rereading helps you read smooooothly. You can activate your reread power to make your reading voice super smooth. You can reread the line. You can reread the page. You can reread the *whole* book, but remember, the smoother the read, the more *alive* everything you read will become!"

TRANSITION TO PARTNER TIME
Readers Read Aloud Using Their Best Reading Voices

"Today during partner time, let's have read-aloud time." The class looked somewhat confused, glancing over at the class schedule, noting that our interactive read-aloud was scheduled for after lunch. "What I mean is, just like when I read aloud books to you, using my very best reading voice, let's have read-aloud time for *you* to read to your partner. You can take turns being the teacher, reading your books to each other in *your* very best reading voices. Quickly, choose some of the books or poems you know really well that you can read (and bring to life) right now during partner time. Now, get started."

Rereading to Bring Our Books to Life

Recruit children to read with smooth voices, lifting the lines of the text off the page.

I put out the familiar rhyme "Rain, Rain, Go Away" while kids began to settle in their spots around the meeting area. Once everyone had gathered I began, "I wonder if we can work to make 'Rain, Rain, Go Away' come to life by activating our reread power. Let's try the first line."

We began to read together, "'Rain, rain, go away.'" I stopped the class to prompt them to reread the line, this time with even stronger fluency. "Readers, that was *pretty* good, but I think we can do even better! Let's reread that line, and remember, we are trying to bring it to life so that it pops right off the page!" We read the line a second time. This time the excited tones came cascading in from kids all over the room.

"Wow, readers! That line really came alive as we reread! You read it so smoothly and dramatically. Let's keep going." We read the next line, "'Come again another day.' We did it, readers! We made that line come to life, but here is a challenge. Can we use reread power and reread to bring the *whole* rhyme to life? Here we go."

The kids reread the whole rhyme with such smooth and passionate voices that they were almost buzzing.

I clutched both hands over my chest. "Readers, that was some of the smoothest reading I have heard, ever! Reread power made your voices smoother than I even knew was possible! Remember, you can activate reread power in your own reading to bring everything you read to life. You can reread to smooth out a line, a page, and even a whole book. Imagine how alive that book will be after all of that rereading. It might even start walking around!"

FIG. 11–1   Be sure that students have access to songs, charts, and poems in the classroom that you have read together, so they can be read independently.

FIG. 11–2   The class calendar is a wonderful resource to practice reading with one-to-one matching, during Morning Meeting or Math, or Reading Workshop.

Readers Use the Pattern to Sing Out Their Books

MINILESSON

IN THIS SESSION, you'll teach children that readers sing out pattern words to help them read smoothly.

CONNECTION

Engage children in marking different rhythms as you read a familiar text.

"Super Readers, can we read 'Rain, Rain Go Away' to start off our workshop? As we read, will you clap your hands like this?" I began to clap a slow rhythm with my hands and began to move my shoulders up and down. "Let's read with this cool beat." We read the song together and then I said, "Let's change it up! Let's reread the poem to *this* beat." I sped up the rhythm and began to snap my fingers. "Wow, we just made 'Rain, Rain, Go Away' the best song ever! We really just brought it to life!"

Compare the students' growing fluency to a symphony.

"I am just *so* proud of you. Yesterday, during reading workshop, I just stopped for a moment and listened." I cupped my hand around my ear. "I listened to the sounds of all of you reading. It was like a reading symphony. It was music to my ears! Your reading voices are getting just a little bit faster and a little bit smoother. I think you're ready to make your reading voices really *sing*!"

❧ **Name the teaching point.**

"Today I want to teach you that one way to read faster and smoother is to realize that knowing the pattern helps you *sing* the words that are the same on every page. Then you can really work at figuring out the words that change."

TEACHING

Demonstrate how you identify the pattern in a familiar text, and sing the repeating words on each page.

"You already know this book well!" I picked up *Brown Bear, Brown Bear*. "Let's make sure that we know what the pattern is and how that can help us sing each of the pages. I bet some of you already know!" Many of the kids nodded, smiling confidently. "That pattern will help us almost *sing* each page. Let's try it." I opened to the first page and read aloud:

> *Brown Bear, Brown Bear,*
>
> *What do you see?*
>
> *I see a red bird*
>
> *looking at me.*
>
> *Red bird, Red bird,*
>
> *What do you see?*
>
> *I see a yellow duck*
>
> *looking at me.*

I looked back toward the class. "Yup! I think I got it. Every page says 'what do you see?' *and* 'I see a _____ looking at me.' But the part that changes is the animal. Okay, so, as I read, I can read that pattern with a beat! I can *sing* the words on that page. Will you sing with me?" I turned the page and led the class in a choral read, scooping up the repeated words of the pattern to practically sing the phrases.

ACTIVE ENGAGEMENT

Introduce a new text, reading aloud the first few pages to allow students to figure out the pattern.

"I'm wondering if *you* can discover the pattern in this new book, *It's Super Mouse!* Listen as I read the first few pages out loud. Thumbs up if you think you realize what the pattern of this book is. What is the same on every page?"

I opened up to the first page and placed it under the document camera. Then, I pointed as I read the first three pages aloud:

> *It's Super Mouse!*
>
> *Super Mouse jumps off a step.*
>
> *Super Mouse jumps off a box.*

You'll want to make a big deal about understanding what is happening in the book to figure out the pattern. Patterns in books are more than just words that repeat. You want students to know that once they know the pattern, they should expect to read those words with more fluency and accuracy; they don't have to approach each page as if it is new.

Draw your students' attention to the words that repeat, inviting students to 'sing' and read with more automaticity. This way, children can devote more attention to the words that change on each page.

I looked up from the book. "Whoa! I *already* see thumbs! Do you think you've figured out how this book goes?" The class nodded. "Quick! Turn and tell your partner how you think the next page will go."

I moved across the room to collect predictions. Most of the class had determined the pattern of the text, and some were making guesses about what Super Mouse would jump off of on the next page.

"I think he's going to jump off a car!" Jordan predicted.

"Yeah, or the roof!" his partner replied.

I coached the pair to say it in a sentence, using the words from the book. "So how will the next page go? Say it like the book. Super Mouse . . ." I waited for the boys to fill in.

"Super Mouse jumps off a car!" "Super Mouse jumps off a roof!" they echoed.

"Maybe! We'll have to turn the page to find out." I moved back to my chair and called the class back. "Readers, eyes back on me. I heard so many of you predict that the next page will probably start like this: 'Super Mouse jumps off a _____.' That seems to be the pattern on each page! Now let's read the next page, find the words that are the same, and *sing* those words. That way we can work on the words that change. Ready?" the class nodded, eager to turn the page and find out if their predictions were accurate.

"A rock!" a bunch of voices called out, noting the illustration.

"Oh! This time it's a rock. Okay, let's use the words that stay the same to read a little faster and smoother right from the start. I pointed under the first word, inviting the class to join in, letting my voice fall out as they read aloud.

LINK

Send children off to read, encouraging them to sing their pattern words and use those patterns to figure out new words.

"So, readers, remember, if you want to help yourself read faster and smoother, you can notice the pattern to help you *sing* the words that are the same. Then you can really work at figuring out the words that change. I can't wait to stop and listen to your reading voices today! I bet it will sound like a whole *choir* of Super Readers reading—and bringing their books to life!"

Readers Use the Pattern to Sing Out Their Books

A S YOU WORK WITH CHILDREN TODAY, you will want not only to support them in "getting through" their books, but also to help them think about the *whole* of a book. Pull together a small group of readers and say to them, "Did you know that the title of your book is another way to help you think about the pattern inside? A title can help readers think about what the book's pattern will be, *and* it can help them say what the book was about—once they're done reading. Let's try. Look at the first book you have. Read the title."

Provide support to those who might need it. Then you might say, "Now think, 'What might each page be about?' Before you read, tell the person sitting next to you." Give children just thirty seconds to do this, and then say, "Okay, now let's read." Here you can coach children to read the page and think back to their prediction. You might ask, "Is what you thought the pattern might be what it actually is?" or "How does this page fit with the title?"

MID-WORKSHOP TEACHING
Figuring Out Tricky Patterns

"Readers, many of you are finding that the patterns in one book and another are not the same! They are different! In *some* of your books, you are finding that the *person* is the *same* on every page, and what that person *does* is *different* on every page. Like this: The mom is reading in the house. The mom is working at her computer. The mom is cleaning in the house. What is changing? That's right, each page has the same person 'The mom is . . .'" and that person is doing something, but on each page she is *doing* something different.

"But in *other* books, the *person or the animal* that does things changes. Listen: The man says hello. The girl says hello. The dog says hello.

"Let's look to see what stays the same and what changes right here on our Super Power chart."

I stood beside the anchor chart and read aloud the first three lines. Students raised their hands to share the pattern. "Yes, that's right! 'We have . . .' and (something) 'power' is on every part of the chart. The part that changes is here, in the middle— the *kind* of power changes.

> **ANCHOR CHART**
>
> ### We Are Super Readers!
>
> - We have pointer power.
> - We have reread power.
> - We have partner power.
> - We have picture power.
> - We have snap word power.
> - We have sound power.
> - We have persistence power.

"Readers have to work extra hard to think, 'What's the pattern here? What's the same on every page? What's different?' Not all your books and songs will have the same pattern. Once you discover the pattern, sing it!"

"It's almost time to read with partners. And all that pattern hunting you did today is really going to help. The pattern can help you *sing* your books as you read together. When you read with your partner today, help them sing out the pattern by telling them what it's going to be, before you even start to read! You can say, 'On every page it goes like this . . .'"

After students have read, prompt them to say what the book was about, using the information in the title to help. Then have them repeat the same steps with the next two books in their baggie.

As you confer with individual readers, you may want to ask them a few questions to assess their thinking about their books. Ask things like "How do these pages go together?" or "What are you noticing that is the same on each page?" You might also assess how well a student is using the pattern to guess the next page or to retell her books. Then give an explicit teaching point to prompt her to synthesize her book or notice more details on the page to help her see how the book fits together. Support ongoing practice by nudging the reader to do this work always. You might say, "What we did right here, you can do in all your books."

After your conference, you may want to share what you just taught with the other students at the table. Say to these readers, "Can I share with you what Rosalind was working on in her book? She was . . ." Show an example from her book and then say, "Can you all try that, right now, with the book you are reading? I am going to come around and listen to you try." Then you can provide some light coaching to the other students at the table as well as notice how the child with whom you were working begins to transfer what you taught her to another book. This allows you to determine the degree to which a student has successfully learned from and applied an individual conference, while simultaneously providing support to additional students in your room.

Chanting Patterns in the Air to Create a Class Book

Use oral rehearsal to plan a class pattern book together, writing sentences in the air.

"Let's play a pattern game to plan our next class book. I'll start, and then when I point to you, tell me how the next page could go. Ready?" I clapped my hands against my lap as I recited the first part of a possible pattern:

> *"We like to read at school!*
>
> *We like to write books at school!*
>
> *We like to . . ."*

I pointed to a student that I knew could carry the pattern with ease, before pointing to another who I suspected would need a tad more repetition before adding on "a page" to our class book. The class filled in possibilities as we wrote our pattern book in the air. Then we chanted it a few times. Afterwards, we wrote the first page to our new class book.

FIG. 12–1   These two kindergartners are reading the class book that they helped write about animals that came to visit their classroom.

Session 13

Readers Use Punctuation to Figure Out *How* to Read

MINILESSON

In your connection, you might tell a story about driving and paying attention to all the traffic signs that tell you to stop or slow down. You might show kids a few photographs of road signs and traffic lights and say, "These signs and lights are almost like a secret code for drivers, letting them know what to do and how to drive."

Then, name the teaching point. "Today I want to teach you that when you want to read a book so the book comes to life for listeners, punctuation is like a secret code, whispering tips about how to read."

In your teaching, you may choose to use a nursery rhyme or poem that features a variety of end punctuation, rather than just periods. For example, you might use "Where Is Thumbkin?" written on chart paper to demonstrate how the question mark changes your reading voice and sounds different than the voice you use to read the lines that end with exclamation points.

Where Is Thumbkin?

Where is Thumbkin?
Where is Thumbkin?
Here I am!
Here I am!
How are you today, sir?
Very well, I thank you.
Run away.
Run away.

During the active engagement, you might ask students to practice reading on in the poem, practicing with a partner before inviting the class to read chorally. Or you may ask students to bring a text from their baggies to practice reading with attention to end punctuation marks. You might voice over, "Be sure to notice those marks at the end of each sentence. Crack the code! What's the period telling you to do? How does the question mark want you to sound? Make your voice match that exclamation point!"

Link today's lesson to the big work of this bend, reminding readers to use all they know to read in ways that bring their books to life, reading and rereading to make their voices smoother. You might say, "Super Readers, be sure to put all your powers together to do everything you can to bring your books to life, reading and *rereading* them to make your voices as smooth as can be. And remember, anytime you read, you can pay close attention to the punctuation, almost like a secret code, thinking, 'How should I read this?'"

CONFERRING AND SMALL-GROUP WORK

As you confer today, you may decide to use shared reading as one of your methods of small-group instruction, offering readers more guided practice with attention to punctuation. You may want to use highlighter tape and ask the group to quickly search the page for punctuation marks before reading. Then, lead the group in a choral reading of the shared text, allowing your voice to drop so that students can do the reading work, but raising your voice if students need a bit more support. You might then coach readers to transfer this same work into their own books, moving from one child to the next, prompting readers by saying things such as "Try that again! Check this punctuation mark." "How should this line sound?" "Listen to me, then you try." "Make your voice sound like you're asking a question." "There's a period here. Take a stop before reading the next sentence."

Mid-Workshop Teaching

For your mid-workshop teaching, you might choose to invite readers on a punctuation hunt. Ask children to hunt for punctuation marks in their books, just like they hunted for word wall words before they started reading. Urge readers to search for the punctuation marks across each page to get themselves ready to change their reading voices as they read each sentence.

Transition to Partner Time

When you transition to partner time, prompt partners to read together, perhaps taking turns being the punctuation police, making sure their partner doesn't speed through the punctuation marks. Readers can remind each other to stop and try it again, this time using the punctuation to signal a stop or a change in intonation.

SHARE

During today's share, you may want to do some interactive writing, using end punctuation to change how sentences sound. You might change the words to "Where Is Thumbkin?" by inserting kids' names and calling kids up to insert the punctuation to end each line of the poem. Then, end the session by inviting the class to read the poem together once more, prompting them to use the punctuation to cue a change in their reading voices.

Readers Change Their Voices to Show They Understand the Book

IN THIS SESSION, you'll teach children that readers use their voices in different ways as they read to show they understand the book. They match their tone to the feelings in the book.

GETTING READY

✔ You will need your demonstration text from yesterday—we used *It's Super Mouse!*, by Phyllis Root (see Teaching and Active Engagement).

✔ Children will need to bring a book, from their book baggie, with them to the rug (see Link).

✔ Tap several children ahead of share time to choose a book to read to the class (see Share).

MINILESSON

CONNECTION

Remind students that storytellers change their voice to match various feelings.

"Readers, do you remember one of our favorite stories about the three billy goats and that mean old troll who lived under the bridge?" The class nodded in unanimous agreement. "Of course you do! You know it *so* well that you're practically storytellers when you read it. You change your voice to sound just like the characters in the story—like that angry troll. How did he sound?"

"Who's that trip-trapping over my bridge?" the children roared, reciting the familiar line.

"Oh my goodness, what *angry* voices! Now, how did the littlest billy goat sound? Did he have the same big, angry voice?"

"No! He was scared!" one student explained.

"Will you show me? Go!" I nudged.

"Please don't take me! I'm too little," a few children joined in with small, feeble voices.

"Oh, yes, that's much different. I understand how the littlest billy goat was feeling just by listening to your voices," I acknowledged. "Reading and rereading your books helps you really know them well so that you can read *all* of your books just like you read *The Three Billy Goats Gruff*."

❧ **Name the teaching point.**

"Today I want to teach you that when you are trying to read a book aloud so that people pull in to listen, it is really important to understand the book, and to be thinking about what it says as you read it. If *you* don't understand it, your listeners won't understand it either."

TEACHING

Model reading pages with a tone that matches the feelings shown in the book.

"I'm going to start reading *It's Super Mouse!* and make sure I know what's happening on each page as I go. I'll need to really make my voice match what's happening on the page so you can understand the book with me. Let me try on the first page."

I opened up the book to page 1, lingering for a moment on the picture before I started to read.

"Hmm, . . . so I see Super Mouse here. He's looking pretty excited with a huge smile on his face and his arm punching up into the air! If Super Mouse looks excited, then I bet I need to make my voice *sound* excited! Let me give it a try. Can you try with me?" I pointed to the first line and we all read together with excitement:

>   *It's Super Mouse!*

"Readers! We did sound excited! I bet people who had never read this book before would know exactly how Super Mouse was feeling. Let's see if we can match Super Mouse's feelings on the next page."

I turned the page and pointed to Super Mouse. "I see a smile! He must be pretty happy jumping off of this step. Let me give it a try." This time, I intentionally read the page with a flat voice that did not reveal any feeling.

>   *Super Mouse jumps off a step.*

"Readers, what do you think? Could you tell Super Mouse was happy after I read the page?"

"No," the class chimed back at me.

"I guess I should try it again. Can you help me?" This time I read with a happy tone.

>   *Super Mouse jumps off a step.*

"That did sound so much happier. Thank you for helping me match Super Mouse's feelings by reading this page in such a happy way."

As your students become stronger at reading words and are more drawn to looking at the print, you will want to make sure that they are still using the pictures and the storylines to help them read. Previewing the page and thinking about what is happening before tackling the print will help prepare readers take on the print more easily. You don't want your readers to become "word callers" and ignore what's happening on each page. Previewing the page will set them up to read the words with more power and meaning.

ACTIVE ENGAGEMENT

Invite children to join you in reading on in the demonstration text, identifying feelings on each page and making their tone match as they read.

"Do you think you could try the next page? Readers, let's look closely at the picture. How do you think Super Mouse is feeling here?" I asked as I pointed at the picture.

Children shouted out various feelings. "Happy!" "Excited!"

"Let's read the page, keeping his feelings in mind." I pointed to each word as the class joined in to read the page.

> *Super Mouse jumps off a hill.*

"You all sound so excited! Even if I couldn't see the page, I could guess what Super Mouse's face would look like. Let's read the next page. Check the picture. Do you have an idea about how we should read it? Thumbs up if you do!"

The children put their thumbs up, and I started to point to each word.

> *Super Mouse flies!*

"We have one last page, readers." I turned the page. "Hmm, . . . Super Mouse looks very different on this last page! What are you thinking? How is Super Mouse feeling here? Turn and tell your partner."

I quickly listened in, hearing various responses from, "He is hurt, so we should sound hurt," to "He looks sad here."

"Readers, many of you noticed that Super Mouse doesn't look excited any more. I guess that means we should change how we read this part. Let's try to read this page and sound hurt or sad. Let's give it a try."

> *OOF! Super Mouse lands.*

"Oh, I could feel the pain in your voices! I bet it's the same pain that Super Mouse felt as he crashed face first into the ground."

FIG. 14–1 Partners can help draw attention to the pictures on the page to notice more details, help solve a word, or help preview the text. Here is a partnership, working together, reading and using the pictures to help them along.

LINK

Direct children to practice bringing their own books to life, using books they have brought with them to the rug.

"Readers, you now know so many different ways to bring your books to life! You can read in a smooooth voice. You know how to make the pattern sing and how to use the punctuation to make the words pop off of the page. Now, you know you can make your voice change to show that you really understand the book. Take out the book you brought with you and use everything you know to make your book come to life!"

I moved around the rug, coaching into various strategies that the kids had learned. I helped remind students of what they had learned on previous days so that they could use each strategy to bring their books to life.

"Wow. The reading that is pouring off of this rug is beautiful! Your books are so alive, I can almost see characters popping off pages and walking around the room. Off you go! Keep bringing books to life!"

Pushing Higher-Level Readers to Tackle New Challenges

YOU'LL WANT TO MAKE SURE you devote some of your conferences and small-group work to push your higher-level readers even higher. At this point in the unit, you'll likely have readers who are reading above benchmark, doing the work of conventional readers in level C texts and beyond. As texts become more complex, you'll want to teach strategies that aim to help your strongest readers tackle these new challenges. For example, you may plan strategy groups that help children read dialogue in their books. Dialogue will become progressively more prevalent in texts starting at level C. Teach readers to notice quotation marks around lines of dialogue and to figure out who is speaking. Then, teach children to reread these lines to sound more like the character. Help them show how the character might say things, using their voices.

While you'll coach the bulk of your readers to point under each word, matching their spoken word to written words, you'll want to start coaching your readers starting at level D to track the print with their eyes, using their finger only at points of difficulty. This will help readers scoop up more words at a time to read with proper phrasing. If a child has difficulty tracking, you might conduct a series of coaching conferences to support the transition. You might coach the child to point and read, and then to reread and sweep, skimming her finger across each line, before rereading once more with her eyes alone.

MID-WORKSHOP TEACHING
Reading to Make Information Sound Interesting

From the middle of the room, I announced, "Attention, all Super Readers who are trying to use all their powers to bring their reading to life. Can I have your eyes and minds on me?" I waited for the students to look up from their books.

"Some of you are noticing that your book doesn't have characters *or* feelings on the page. Like in this book about pigs." I held it up. "*How* do you change your voice to show the feeling when it's just a pig just doing some stuff?

"Well, I am here to tell you that you can read that kind of book, just like a teacher would, in the most interested-sounding voice. Listen to how I read these pages with an interested voice."

After reading a couple of pages I said, "Did you hear how I did that with my voice? I tried to make the information sound just so, so interesting! I changed the sound of my voice, making some words softer, and I kind of gave other words like a strong punch, and said them stronger.

"As you continue to read your books, you can show the feeling in your book or make your voice sound interesting to read information! Make parts softer or give some words an extra punch!"

TRANSITION TO PARTNER TIME
Challenge partners to read the same book and change their voices in different ways to bring the book alive.

"Super Readers, as you decide *how* you will read your book, remember, you can reread your book a couple of different ways. Partner 1 can read her book, changing *her* voice to make it come to life, and then Partner 2 can reread that *same* book, changing *his* voice to bring it to life. Maybe it will be the *same* or maybe you will do it in a *different* way!

"Go ahead, start reading, Partner 1. Afterward, let Partner 2 take a turn with your book. Then it's Partner 2's turn to choose a book. Keep going, back and forth, until it's share time! I bet you two will be able to read a whole bunch of books from your baggies!"

Using Children's Read-Alouds to Model Reading in Different Ways

Choose several students to model their reading in different ways.

"Readers, I chose several of you today, for our teaching share, to lead us as a class in some reading of *your* books! I asked a few of you to choose your best book, the one you think you would like to share, and asked you to think about *how* the class should read it and bring it to life! Ori is going to go first. What book are you going to lead us in reading?"

"*I Play Soccer!*" Ori said, and he put his book under the document camera."

"Okay, go stand by the screen and take the pointer with you. Tell us, how shall we read? At the same time, echo reading, or see-saw reading?"

"Echo reading!"

"Wonderful! Let's bring this book to life! Everyone get your voices ready." Ori began, and the class echoed his reading. At times I needed to assist Ori in his reading, but at other times, I chimed in with the class. "Super job, Super Readers. Now, Mia is ready to lead the class. What book did you pick?"

Super Readers Talk about Books, Too!

IN THIS SESSION, you'll teach children that readers not only read books, they talk about them, too, to bring them to life.

GETTING READY

✔ Make your "We Are Super Readers!" chart accessible for you to refer to, and have the strategy "We have book talk power." ready to add to the chart (see Connection and Link).

✔ Use a familiar text in your demonstration. We use *It's Super Mouse,* by Phyllis Root (see Teaching).

✔ Ask students to bring one book from their book baggies (see Active Engagement).

✔ Create a message from Reader-Man that presents a challenge to students (see Conferring).

✔ Prepare baggies for a small group with excerpts from familiar books (not the entire text). The baggies should contain photocopied pictures from a book and the matching text written on sentence strips and cut up into parts (see Conferring and Mid-Workshop Teaching).

✔ Private/Partner Reading sign (see Transition to Partner Time).

✔ Gather together several class interactive-writing books (see Share).

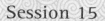

MINILESSON

CONNECTION

Energize children around their abilities to bring books to life.

"Readers, it feels like books are coming to life all over this room. They're practically crawling out of your baggies and jumping out of the baskets in our library. You are using all of your super reading powers to read the words *and* make your reading voices *sing* those words. The more you reread your books, the more you understand those books, and the more alive the stories become.

"But here's the thing. It's not just the words and your reading voices that bring those stories to life. All the ways you talk about books bring them to life, too."

❖ **Name the teaching point.**

"Today I want to teach you that Super Readers don't just *read* books, they *talk* about books, too. You can activate your *book talk* power. One way to get your book talk started is to introduce your book to your partner before you read it together."

Add to the chart:

- **We have book talk power.**

GRADE K: SUPER POWERS

TEACHING

Demonstrate a nonexample by skipping the book introduction and jumping right to reading the first page.

"You can activate that book talk power before you even start to read with your partner. You can introduce the book you'll read first. Can I introduce you to a book right now?" The kids nodded. "Everyone, pretend you are my partner and partner time is just about to start."

I put my copy of *It's Super Mouse!* under the document camera and quickly mumbled, "Let's read this book." I flipped hastily to the first page and started reading.

"No! No! No!" several kids scolded. "You have to *talk* first."

"Oh! My goodness, how could I forget? I was so excited to *read* it, I forgot to activate book talk power! That can happen a lot, Super Readers, so it's your job to power up and remember to talk *before* you start reading. Okay, let me try again." I flipped back to the cover of the book.

Rely on the students to fill in important details to add onto your book introduction. Then, model a strong introduction to provide the class with an exemplar.

"This book is called *It's Super Mouse!* This is Super Mouse right here. He wears a cape and a mask and . . ." I tapped my chin, as if struggling to fill in more details. "Can you help me? Maybe we can think about how the pages go to tell a little bit more about the book. Turn and tell your partner what else we can say to introduce this book." I leaned in to collect a few ideas before voicing back possibilities.

"Oh! I heard some important details I should add to introduce this book. Okay, let me start again. Ahem! This book is called *It's Super Mouse!* This is Super Mouse right here. He wears a cape and a mask, and on every page he jumps off something. But something *bad* happens at the end. Let's read it together to find out what happens!" I changed my tone to address the class, "Better?" Thumbs went up and some children clapped their hands. I did a curtsy.

"Did you see how I activated my book talk power to introduce the book *before* reading it? You can use the title and the picture on the cover to talk *and* you can think about how the pages go together—the pattern of the book—to explain how the book goes."

ACTIVE ENGAGEMENT

Coach readers to rehearse and give book introductions using a book they know.

"Will you take out the book you brought with you today? Since it's a book you *already* read and know, think about how you might introduce it to someone. Plan what you'll say. Whisper it to yourself right now." I cupped my hands over my mouth as if whispering a secret.

This minilesson provides opportunities for your students to strengthen both their retelling skills and their oral language. While this unit emphasizes foundational skills, you will want to be sure that you balance your teaching by helping students build meaning as they read. Book talk is a wonderful way to tackle both.

Be sure to listen in as students give book introductions to partners. You'll want to assess how much your students understand and remember as they read.

FIG. 15–1 Readers' comments: "This book is about Carla. She goes on a waterslide and splashes!" "Carla goes to the waterslide and she climbs up the ladder and is a little nervous. But then she goes down the slide and splashes in the water and loves it!"

As kids rehearsed their book introductions, I voiced over to coach them along, "What's the book called? How do the pages go? What's the same on every page?" After a moment or so, I gathered the students' attention. "Okay, Super Readers. Are you ready to activate your book talk power? Ready? Partner 1, you start first. Go!"

I moved around the rug, listening in and coaching some partners to include more detail and others to refrain from reciting every page. "Okay, Partner 2, your turn. Go!"

LINK

Choral read the "We Are Super Readers!" chart to remind children of all the ways they can bring books to life.

"Super Readers, remember, you can *read* and *talk* about your books to bring them to life. You can introduce your books to your partner before you read them together. Let's read the chart together so that you can remember to use *everything* you can to bring your books to life." I led the class in a choral reading of the anchor chart before sending kids off to start private reading.

FIG. 15–2 Examples of charts for super powers and partnerships

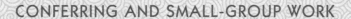

Putting It All Together: Integrating Meaning, Structure, and Visual Cues

TODAY you might pull a small group of students who need practice integrating print with the meaning of the text. Say to them, "Super Readers, you aren't going to believe this. I got a text message last night from Reader-Man! This is what it said." You might want to add to the drama by reading a mock text from your phone:

Hello, my Super Reader friends.

I've got a problem for you to mend.

It's Reader-Man here,

There is nothing to fear!

To test your powers, and see if they're strong,

Here's a mission for you to go on!

I took some words from one of your books

And threw them around without a look.

Now, they're left and right and up and down.

Look at your teacher—she has such a frown!

So, power up, Readers! I need your brains!

Please take those words and rearrange!

Take what is jumbled and make it sound great.

Use ALL your powers! Ready . . . ACTIVATE!

Give each child a baggie that contains cut-up parts of a text—excerpts from a familiar book (not the entire text). The baggies should contain photocopied pictures from a

MID-WORKSHOP TEACHING   Readers Plan for Partner Time: Marking Pages to Talk About

"Readers, when you read a book really well, making the book come to life, then you find yourself thinking about the book, and pretty soon you just *have* to put the book down to talk about it. If that happens to you, instead of interrupting your partner, you can mark the page with a Post-it so you remember to talk about it during partner time.

"You can use private time to get ready for partner time. You can mark pages you want to talk about. Maybe it's a page you want to give your partner a peek at when you introduce it. *Or* maybe it's a page that you think is silly or sad. You can use a Post-it to remember to share it with your partner. Then, you can read and talk about it together. I've put Post-its in your baggies. Try it now!"

TRANSITION TO PARTNER TIME   Remind kids to introduce their book to their partner before starting to read it.

I moved to the class Private Reading sign and flipped it to read Partner Reading. "Boys and girls, it's time to huddle up to read and *talk* with your partners. Get into partner position: side by side, book in the middle." I waited for partners to transition before giving the class a clear direction. "Now, you know that one way to activate your book talk power is by introducing your book *before* you read it together. Make sure not to jump right into your books! Say what your book is called and what it's about. You can even use the pattern to explain how the book goes. Then, you can read it together, *and* when you get to a page that's marked with a Post-it you can stop and book talk some *more*! Super Readers can talk and read and talk and read. Get started!"

book, with the matching text written on sentence strips and cut apart. You might say, "That Reader-Man! Can you believe he mixed up our books? Readers, today it is our job to use all our powers to put the story back together. Readers, let's power up!" Guide students as they get to work putting the story back together in order. Afterward, students can check their work by reading the original shared reading text. Make note of students who continue to have difficulty integrating meaning, structure, and visual cues. This information will help guide your conferences and small-group instruction going forward.

You may also decide to pull a group of higher-level readers who need support with more complex word-solving skills. These students are most likely working on integrating meaning, structure, and visual sources of information as they read, as well as self-correcting any miscues as they read. These readers will also draw on known parts of words to read.

Pull together a group of readers at similar levels to introduce a new text that is just a notch above their just-right book level. Give these students a quick book introduction and instead of giving each student a copy of the book, as you would in a guided reading session, give one book to each pair.

As students read, coach partners to prompt the reader to solve words or fix errors. Coach readers to use MSV, checking the picture, thinking about the language structure of the text, and checking across the word for known parts.

Prompt partners to retell the book together. Then give both partners a quick teaching point. You might then have students reread that book, using and practicing the strategy you just taught.

Remind students that they can continue to do this work in *all* of their books. You may leave the group, encouraging partnerships to continue this work together. Tell them to start with the ones that they haven't read yet, or that they have read the least amount of times, as a way of moving gradually toward more challenging texts.

Don't Give Away the Whole Book!

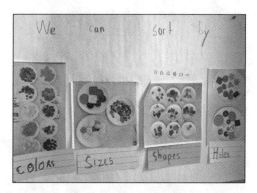

Point out to children that book introductions do not give away the ending.

"Readers, thumbs up if you remembered to introduce your books to your partner before you read them together!" The children held up their thumbs. "Wonderful! Those introductions help your partner get to know your book a little bit better. It's a lot like introducing a movie before you watch it or introducing a game before you play it. That book introduction even helps you read it so much better because you know a little bit about how the book goes. But here's something important to remember: don't give the *whole* book away!

"Can you imagine going to a movie and someone tells you what happens at the end! It would ruin the surprise! It might even make you feel like not watching the movie at all." I gasped in despair.

Engage partners in introducing a class book without giving away the ending.

"So right now, let's practice introducing some of our class books, remembering to not give the *whole* book away." I held up a copy of one of the class books written during interactive writing. "Do you remember this one?" The children nodded. "Let me reread it quickly. Think about how it goes and what you might say to introduce it." I reread each page:

Superheroes!

Look at Superman fly.

Look at Wonder Woman jump and run.

Look at Spiderman climb.

Look at Batman drive fast.

Look at Reader Man point and read.

We are Super Readers. We have powers, too!

"Introduce it! Remember to say the title and how it goes, but don't give away the ending!"

"Now let's try it with this book," I held up another class book and gave the class an opportunity to practice again.

FIG. 15–3 You may decide to make various types of interactive writing texts with your students, such as the chart and diagram shown here, that they can enjoy returning to read during reading workshop.

Readers Retell Books after They Read Them

MINILESSON

In your connection, you might tell the story of leaving a movie theater with friends and talking about all the different parts of the movie—funny parts, confusing parts, surprising parts. Compare this to the thinking and talking readers do after they finish a book.

Then, name the teaching point. "Today I'm going to teach you that when you read a book well, you end up seeing things in the book that seem important. Maybe you see things that are surprising or that are funny. When you finish a book, sometimes you want to talk about it by retelling it to your partner.

In your teaching, you might return to *It's Super Mouse!* to demonstrate how you can turn back through the pages to retell the book. Start by rereading the final few pages to demonstrate how readers linger after they've finished a book to remember all the parts, rather than moving quickly to a new book. You might say, "Wait! Before we read another book together, let's remember to activate book talk power by retelling it! Let's go back through the pages of *It's Super Mouse!* to talk about what happened in the story by retelling it." Teach children to use the title and the pattern to retell how the pages go (rather than retelling every single page), using the same structure you provided to help kids introduce their book. Coach readers to say, "This book is called . . . and on every page . . ." and then to fill in the ending. Help kids consider how the ending fits with the title or the pattern. For example, you might demonstrate how to retell *It's Super Mouse!* You might say, "This book is called *It's Super Mouse!* On every page, Super Mouse jumps off something. But at the end, Super Mouse falls down! The ending is a surprise because it's the opposite of what happens on every page. Instead of jumping up, Super Mouse falls down." Don't wait to get kids active. Prompt students to think alongside you. Say, "I bet you're remembering all these parts too!"

During the active engagement, you might choose to prompt partners to continue retelling the demonstration text. "Quick, try retelling this book again with your partner!" you might say.

If needed, you can turn the pages of *It's Super Mouse!* to help students remember the sequence of the book. Alternatively, you might prepare for today's active engagement by asking children to bring a book they have already read to the rug before you start the lesson. Ask partners to retell those books.

Link today's lesson to *all* the important work readers do to understand their books well. Remind students that readers read with voices that show what's happening and use the pattern to introduce and help retell their books when they are finished.

As you work with students in small groups today, you may extend that work by helping students with their ability to retell. For students who have difficulty with retelling, you may need to show them how to retell using their fingers as a guide, or let four students be "story builders," each retelling only a specific part of a familiar text. You might say, "Readers, when we retell, it's sometimes helpful to use our fingers as a guide. Let's retell this book, *Brown Bear, Brown Bear* together!" Guide students to use the title and the pattern structure demonstrated in the minilesson to aid in their retellings. Coach them individually as they retell their part of the story, giving students back their words in logical order for clarity. "Tell me if I have this right, Alex," you might say.

Mid–Workshop Teaching

For your mid-workshop teaching, you might extend how students talk about books by adding a "pinch of you" to say what you think. You might say, "Remember the way you stopped on each page of your learn-about-the-world books to 'add a pinch of you' to say what you think? You can add a pinch of you when you retell a book too! Maybe you see things that are surprising or that are funny or that make you sad, even. When you finish a book, sometimes you just have to talk more about it and say, 'Did you notice . . .' or 'Wasn't it funny how . . .' or 'I was so surprised when . . .'" Remember, you can always add 'a pinch of you' to say what you think about the book."

Transition to Partner Time

When you transition to partner time, prompt partners to put everything they know together. Remind students to introduce their books before they read; then, use the pattern to make their reading voices smooth *and* change their voices to match what's happening on each page; then, go back and retell the book when they finish reading.

SHARE

During today's share, coach partners to talk *more* about their books, extending the work they do to say, "I think . . ." by teaching them to elaborate on their ideas, using the word *because* to say more. Remind children of what they learned in the previous unit to back up their "I thinks" using the picture. Then, teach children that another way to back up their ideas is to explain *why*. Get kids practicing with partners on the rug, going back to one of the books they read and talked about, this time using the word *because* to say more about their reactions to each page.

Celebration: The Gift of Reading

MINILESSON

IN THIS SESSION, you'll teach children that readers share their gift of reading by reading to others.

CONNECTION

Tell children that they have something to give back to their families in exchange for the reading lives they've been given.

"So far, most of your reading lives have come from what other people have given you. You've been taken to the library and given books that you love. You've been pulled onto laps and into chairs to snuggle around stories. Thumbs up if every night you listen to a bedtime story." Many children held up their thumbs. "Here in school, you've been read to, too, and of course, you've read along with one another. And now, you've spent the past week and a half bringing your stories to life!

"Well guess what? You now have something to give back."

❧ **Name the teaching point.**

"Today I want to teach you that you can give the gift of reading! You can think about the people you love and which stories they would love to hear. You can decide *who* you'll read to, *what* you'll read, and *how* you'll read it."

TEACHING AND ACTIVE ENGAGEMENT

Model how you think about an audience that you want to share a book with, and then decide which book to perform and how.

"Readers, today you'll work really hard to make a reading performance that's as strong as it can be, and then, you'll have the chance to give the gift of reading to the people who matter most to you—your family. For a little while, we will transform our reading workshop into a gift workshop. So, let's get to work making our gifts!"

GETTING READY

- ✔ Choose a book from your library to demonstrate reading with expression (see Teaching and Active Engagement and Share).

- ✔ Children will need to bring their book baggies to the rug (see Active Engagement and Share).

- ✔ Display both the "We Are Super Readers!" and the "Readers Read with a Partner" charts (see Teaching and Active Engagement and Link and Transition to Partner Time).

- ✔ Ask students to bring their books or gifts to the meeting area to share with a small group (see Share).

"First, though, you'll need to pick an audience and a book. Let me show you how I do this.

"Let's see. My dad was a really big influence on my reading life. I remember sitting on his lap while he told me made-up stories about a little girl and the adventures she had with her horse. Every night, this girl and her horse went on a new adventure together, and as they galloped, my dad would move his legs up and down so that it felt like I was actually riding!

"I loved those stories. You know what? I think my dad would enjoy an exciting story, like this one," I said, and held up a book from the class library. "It has lots of action! Listen as I practice reading it in my very best reading voice." I stood up and read a couple pages out loud, using my voice and gestures to convey the action.

Invite children to choose an audience for their gift of reading and some possible books to share.

"Right now, will you think, '*Who* will I give a gift of reading? Who will be my audience?'" I waited as children pondered their options. "It might be someone at home or a friend or someone in our school or even a favorite toy!

"Now think, 'What will I read? What might they love to hear?' I'm sure you'll come up with *lots* of choices. When you have some books and poems and songs in mind, take them out of your book baggie and place them on your lap."

Suggest that partners work together to practice reading their books and giving each other tips, referring to the anchor charts.

Once I saw that all children had made selections I said, "Right now, will you turn and practice with your partner? Partner 2, you go first. Tell Partner 1 *who* you'll read to and *what* you'll read to them. You can even explain *why* you chose those books or poems. Then practice *how* you'll read it, making sure to use your very best performing voice—with lots of expression. And Partner 1, your job is to be helpful. Look at our charts," I pointed to the two anchor charts, "so that you can give helpful reminders."

Children have worked hard to bring their books to life throughout this bend, and now you'll give them a chance to show off their fluency and comprehension skills. Meanwhile, you give them an even bigger purpose for this work: to perform a book for family—to give back the gift of reading.

You will want to have both charts on display during this lesson. As you watch and listen to your students read, refer back to the charts and give brief voice-overs to coach the group as they read. You might offer tips such as: "Don't forget to pay attention to the punctuation." "See the period at the end? That means you need to stop and take a breath before you read the next sentence." "Oh, a pattern! Remember how it helps to sing out those words that are the same on every page." "Think about what's happening and then make your voice show that big feeling." "Be my echo. Listen to me. Then, you try."

"You might say, 'Don't forget to use pointer power!' Then switch. Get started!"

As children worked, I crouched low and listened in to as many partnerships as I could in the few minutes I'd allotted for this activity, offering coaching tips here and there:

LINK

Ask children to settle on one book to perform and then send them off to practice reading the book on their own.

"Instead of reading *everything* you can today, practice reading the book or the poem you'll perform. As you do, you might set a little goal for yourself. Maybe you want to work on a couple of your super powers—like pointer power to give every word one tap and picture power to read the part that changes." I pointed to the anchor charts as I reviewed a couple of strategies. "And you'll definitely use reread power to practice using your voice to bring your books to life. Ready to work on making your reading stronger and stronger so you can give it as a gift? Off you go!"

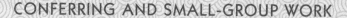

Supporting Students in Preparing for Their Gift of Reading

AS CHILDREN READ THE TEXTS they've selected, move around the room, helping them set goals for their performances and put finishing touches on these "gifts." Some students may decide that they will focus on reading more smoothly, singing out the patterns as they read. Others might show off their super reading powers, emphasizing how they use these to read. You might encourage children to plan for turn-and-talks during their performances. They can use Post-its to mark places where they might stop reading and engage in an interaction with their gift recipient. Maybe they'll point out details in their pictures, make sound effects or facial expressions to communicate meaning, or read certain pages or parts more than once. They could revisit previously read pages, especially when the current page connects with the prior ones in some important way. They could stop to say what they are thinking about at a certain part, and they could ask their listener to share what he is thinking, too. This is an effective way to teach the crucial concept that readers think while they are reading, thereby discovering meaning.

Extend the idea that partners help each other by suggesting that readers can be their own partners, helping themselves. One way readers do this is by self-monitoring and using fix-up strategies. Once you have reminded children to self-monitor, they also

MID-WORKSHOP TEACHING
Trying Out Different Ways to Perform a Book

"Readers, eyes up here a minute. I have a tip for you. As performers get ready to share the gift of reading, they have decisions to make. Decide what voices you'll use to read the words and what parts you will act out with your *whole* body. Performers try out different ways to figure out how to share their book with an audience! Right now, try a new way to read your book."

TRANSITION TO PARTNER TIME   **Invite kids to use all their reading powers as they read with a partner.**

"Readers, it's time to read with your partner! You can practice together to get ready to give your reading gifts! When you get together, share the goals you set and then help each other reach the goal. Partner 1, this time you go first. Partner 2, give helpful reminders. Ask questions or give little tips, like 'Activate reread power! Read the page again.'" I pointed to the "We Are Super Readers!" chart.

ANCHOR CHART

We Are Super Readers!

- We have pointer power.
- We have reread power.
- We have partner power.
- We have picture power.
- We have snap word power.
- We have sound power.
- We have persistence power.
- We have book talk power.

"Then switch. Work together to get your reading gift ready."

need to self-correct. You might say to your kindergartners, "When you are giving the gift of reading, you need to make sure that it is as beautiful as possible. Sometimes, though, it will not be perfect. You will mess up. But that's okay because you can use your reread power to fix it. Your listener will understand. Messing up happens to everyone. You will just need to say, 'Oops, let me try that again,' and then reread that whole sentence or page."

Remind children of the ways they've learned to tackle tricky words, and tell them that self-corrections are one of the most important signs that they are growing as readers. So many students do not fix up their reading; they just ignore the errors. Reinforcing self-correcting as both a behavior and a reading strategy will prepare them to move up to texts of higher complexity.

As you help children prepare for the celebration, you will, of course, remind them of all that they have learned this year. They can reread a specific line on a page, trying out different ways it might sound. They might make a line or a word louder or softer; they might try a line slower or faster. They can think about whether it sounds better to take big breaths or little breaths in between words as they read. Children can pretend to be each other's audience and offer tips as they listen. You might also remind them to slow down to notice more in the pictures, mark "wow" places to talk about, or tell how all the pages go together, also reinforcing the thinking students have learned to do in their books this year.

Giving the Gift of Reading

Welcome children to the final celebration and invite two sets of partners to team up, taking turns performing and being an audience. Remind them of their jobs in each role.

When children had gathered on the rug, I said, "Readers, when I look at you, I no longer see the little kids you were at the start of this unit. I see big, strong Super Readers! You've worked so hard to master one power after another, to use *all* of your super powers to read *everything* you can!

"Are you ready to celebrate the gift of reading? Later, you'll give this gift to someone at home or at school. Right now, though, let's give these gifts to friends in our classroom! Will you and your partner turn and face another pair of partners?" I helped them get into groups of four, and then said, "Listeners, remember that you have a job to do. Your job is to be the *best* listener. You might laugh at a funny part or cover your mouth when you're surprised by something. And, of course, you'll make sure to keep your eyes on the reader. I bet you'll even clap at the end!

"And, performers, here are a few tips: before you begin your reading, show your audience the cover of your book and introduce it, just like you do when you meet during partner time." I held up *The Little Engine that Could* and said, "I might say, 'This book, *The Little Engine that Could*, is about a train that tries to get over the side of the mountain so it can deliver gifts to children.'

"And at the end of the book, will you just slap the book closed and return to your spot? No way! You might say, 'Did you notice how . . .' or 'Weren't you surprised when . . .' Remember to activate your book talk power and add a pinch of you to say what you think! Okay, let the celebration begin!"

Walk around the room, listening in and admiring children's readings. Then tell them they are ready to share this gift with others—and encourage them to do this often.

As children performed, I made the rounds, giving appreciative nods and gestures to show that I admired what they were doing. Then I convened the class's attention and said, "Bravo! You truly are Super Readers. You are ready to give the gift of reading to others. If you're giving this gift to someone at home, you'll want to make sure you take your book or poem home tonight. This is a very special gift. And you know what? I hope that you don't just give it once. Keep on giving the gift of reading, with other books and other friends and family."

Read-Aloud

Getting Ready: BOOK SELECTION

For your interactive read-alouds across this unit, you'll want to choose picture books that feature engaging characters and strong story language, much like the emergent storybooks you read across the last unit. Reading aloud exposes children to richer literature than the texts they are reading independently. While your *shared* reading is aimed to give students access to texts just a notch above their independent reading level, your *read-aloud* texts should expose young readers to texts that are much more complex. Choose picture books that are similar to Kevin Henkes' *Wemberly Worried*, Rosemary Wells' *Yoko*, or Audrey Penn's *The Kissing Hand*.

We chose *So Much!*, by Trish Cooke, because it celebrates the love of family, something young children will quickly relate to. The rhythm of the text quickly hooks listeners as they meet all the aunts and uncles and cousins and grandparents who all love the baby *so much*. You'll probably notice children chime in as you read the repetitive phrases across the story. This story will easily become a favorite and one that you'll reread time and time again across the month and year.

You might choose to pair your picture book read-aloud with information texts to create a text set, perhaps one that is even linked to your content area study in science or social studies. *It's Okay to Be Different* and *The Family Book*, by Todd Parr, continue your focus on families, a topic that many kindergarten classrooms start off the school year studying during social studies. While both are patterned list books, they're certainly written at a text level that will be above *most* if not *all* of your readers. These

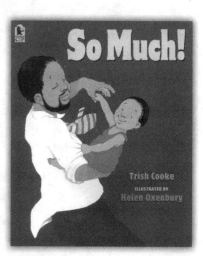

So Much!, by Trish Cooke, illustrated by Helen Oxenbury

texts will also create quite a bit of discussion. You will be able to build similar skills across these books as well as deepen students' understanding about themselves. In any case, you, too, can choose and select a series or group of books by the same author or on the same topic that will allow students to work not only on similar skills, but to build content around a variety of subjects.

READ-ALOUD SESSION 1

BEFORE YOU READ

Introduce the book by giving students the gist of the story and taking a picture walk of the first few pages.

"This is a story called *So Much!* It's written by Trish Cooke and illustrated by Helen Oxenbury. This story is about a great big family who have all come to see the baby. They love the baby *so much*! Let's take a picture walk to peek at a few pictures and find out who might come to visit and what they do when they see the baby." Scan over a few pages, perhaps through page 7, recruiting the kids to say aloud what they see in ways that construct the gist of the story.

Page numbers are cited using the first page of text, starting with "They weren't doing anything," as page 1.

Page 1: Point to the picture to recruit readers to say who's in the scene and what's happening.

"There's the baby! Who's this? Yes, that must be Mom. Oh, and I see the word *Mom* right here. What are they doing? You're right. They're kind of just sitting on the couch, maybe they're staring out the window. I wonder why. Hmm, . . . That's true! Maybe they're waiting for guests to arrive!"

Pages 2–7: Recruit kids to figure out who the new character might be and what she might be saying and doing. Then, prompt a prediction.

"Who might this be? I think this is the baby's auntie. I wonder what she's saying. Yes, maybe. Maybe she's telling him to give her a big hug. I see her hands open wide." Turn the page. "Oh, and now what are they doing?" Have students fill in. "That looks like fun!" Turn the page. "Oh! They're all back on the couch, sitting again. What do you think will happen next? Turn and tell your partner." Listen in to students' responses to quickly assess predictions.

- Are students predicting the very next action?

- Are students predicting a series of events?

- Are students using the pattern to predict?

Auntie—
Auntie Bibba.
Auntie Bibba came inside with her
arms out wide, wide, wide
and one big, big smile.

"Oooooooh!" she said.
"I want to squeeze him,
I want to squeeze the baby,
I want to squeeze him
SO MUCH!"

AS YOU READ

Read the text with expression, emphasizing the rhythm and repetition of the text.

As you open the book and begin to read, be sure to read in a way that brings out the feeling and personality of each new character. For example, you might move from a listless reading of the start of the first page, until the doorbell rings. Then, bring out the affectionate tone of Auntie Bibba on the following pages.

Page 13: Prompt children to check their predictions by retelling what's happened so far.

Get children to accumulate the story before reading on and to think about how the characters' feelings have changed. You might prompt students to turn and talk. Say, "Let's stop and think, 'What's happened so far? Does it match what you thought would happen?' Turn and talk about what's happened so far in the story. Retell together." You might voice back a retell, highlighting the pattern of the story. Then, prompt students to anticipate what might happen next, making another prediction.

Page 14: Pause after reading the text to study the illustration and build meaning. Urge children to act it out to support understanding.

"Hmm, . . . this is Nannie and Gran-Gran. I'm learning that the baby has *two* grandmas. Look at them here. They have their handbags hanging on one arm, like this." Position your arm to act it out. "And they have their 'brella hook up on their sleeve.' Huh?" Demonstrate how you study the picture to build meaning. "Oh! They have their umbrella hooked to their arm. See it here in the picture? Okay, let's be Nannie and Gran-Gran walking into the house with our handbag and umbrella. Act it out with me. Let's all say, 'Yoooooo hoooooo!' What else might they be saying?"

Pages 15–16: Think aloud before prompting students to turn and talk to share ideas.

"I notice the grandmas singing and dancing with the baby. They have great big smiles. Even the baby is smiling and dancing. I think they love each other *so much*." Leave a space for kids to fill in with their own ideas. Then, turn the page to read on. At the end of page 16, you might say, "Will you turn and tell your partner what *you* notice and think? Remember to use our 'Readers Talk about Books' chart to say, 'I notice . . .' and 'I think . . .' to share with your partner."

SESSION 1: AS YOU READ

p. 14: Pause after reading to study the illustration and build meaning. Urge children to act it out to support understanding.

"Huh? What does this mean? Let's check the picture for clues. Now let's act it out so that we understand what's happening here."

ANCHOR CHART

Readers TALK about Books

"I notice . . ."
"I think . . ."
"I wonder . . ."
"What do you think?"

Listen in, once again, to assess students' thinking, as well as their speaking and listening skills.

- Are students taking turns?

- Are students listening to each other?

- Are students using the picture/words to say what they notice?

- Are students sharing ideas? Asking questions?

Pages 20–22: Stop to clarify meaning.

"'I want to fight him, I want to fight the baby, I want to fight him *so much!*' Oh, no! Does Cousin Kay-Kay *really* want to fight the *baby?* I feel worried." Elicit a few responses, and then quickly read on to the next page. "Oh! They're being playful. It's silly fighting and wrestling. Phew!"

Page 24: Prompt children to consider what characters are saying or thinking.

"Who do you think they're waiting for? I wonder what they're saying or thinking right now. Hmm, . . ." Give children some wait time to fill in possibilities. "Quick, turn and tell your partner. Say, 'I think . . .'" Gesture back to the "Readers TALK about Books" chart. Be sure to voice back several responses to help children understand that there is not one correct answer, but that readers can have many different ideas. "I heard *lots* of ideas about what they might be saying or thinking right now. Maybe they're thinking, 'Who's at the door?' or maybe the cousins over here are saying, 'I can't see!' Or maybe Mom is saying, 'Come in!' Let's read and find out who it is." Stop to check predictions to confirm or revise. Then, read to the end of the story.

AFTER YOU READ

Remind kids to stick with the book after they finish reading.

"What a great story. It reminds me of my family and how we crowd in the house to have big dinners and celebrate special days. Thumbs up if it makes you think about special times and special people in your family! Let's stick with this book in our minds a little longer!" You might engage in a whole-class conversation first, helping children retell the story together.

Quickly retell the key details as a class to support comprehension of the text.

"Let's turn back to the beginning and think about all the parts of this story to retell what happened in *So Much!* What happened first?" Flip back to the first few pages to help children recall the events in order. "Yes! Mom and the baby were on the couch not doing anything really, and then the doorbell rang! What happened next? Turn and retell with your partner."

SESSION 1: AS YOU READ

pp. 20-22: Stop to clarify meaning.

"Wait! What's happening here? Why did the character do/say that? Turn and tell your partner what you're thinking."

Listen in to students' retell before reconvening to name back key details.

"I heard you say Auntie Bibba came in and she wanted to squeeze the baby and she read him a book. Then, what happened next?" Listen in to partnerships, then voice back the next part of the retell. "After that, the uncle came and he kissed the baby. Then, the grandmas came and danced with the baby. *So* many people came. What happened at the end? Yes! They surprised Daddy for his birthday, then everyone went home, and the baby went to bed remembering how everyone loves him *so much*."

Coach students to practice their retell. "Let's put all the parts together to retell the *whole* story all the way through. Retell what happened at the beginning, then what happened next, and after that and at the end. Go!"

Afterwards, ask students to talk about their ideas, feelings, and other connections they have with the story.

SESSION 2

BEFORE YOU READ

Set students up to listen with a new lens as you reread.

Remind students of the gist of the story. You might say, "Boys and girls, we all know *So Much!* is about a *big* family who is coming over for a surprise birthday party for the dad. But the most important thing to know is that they love the baby *so much*. Well, I love this book *so much* that I can't wait to read it again. Let's activate *reread power*, and this time, let's work hard to notice even more about the pictures to learn more about the characters and story." You might, instead, choose to give students more responsibility for recalling the details of the text, asking them to retell what they remember as you fill in missing details.

AS YOU READ

Reread the text with expression, pausing to study the illustrations a bit more closely to see new details.

You'll want to think aloud, as if noticing a new detail, to reinforce one purpose of rereading and urge children to do the same work across the read-aloud. On the first page, you might read and then stop to realize what's happening in the illustration based on your stronger understanding of the whole story. "Oh! The first time we read this I wasn't quite sure what they were doing on the couch, but now I realize they're waiting for the guests to arrive. They're probably peeking out the window to see if anyone's coming."

Page 11: Stop to think more deeply about the characters.

"Let's study Auntie Bibba and Uncle Didi. How do you think they feel? How do you know?" Prompt readers to use the picture to think about the characters. Listen in and coach partners while they turn and talk. Then, call students back to add on to their responses. You might say, "So, Auntie Bibba squeezes the baby and bounces him on her knee and reads him a book, and Uncle Didi kisses him and rocks him on his shoulders. I'm thinking the baby must really love all of that attention. I bet he loves his auntie and uncle *so much*, too."

Page 13: Prompt children to chime in with you, reciting the repetitive phrases across the pages.

"I bet you know the parts of this book *so* well you could jump in and help me read some of the words." Place the text under a document camera to enlarge the print. Read the first paragraph, slowing down at "nothing really . . ." to urge kids to fill in: "Then, DING DONG!" You might continue to urge children to chime in across the remainder of the read.

Page 24: Stop to clarify meaning.

Read to the end of the page, and then stop to reread the last line, "'Mom said, "What craziness all around!"' What does that mean? What's happening here? Turn and tell your partner." Once children have shared in pairs, voice back what you heard to help them better understand the story. "I am hearing some of you say that everyone is really busy playing and talking and listening to music. There's a lot happening in the house. There's *so much* noise and there's *so much* love, too."

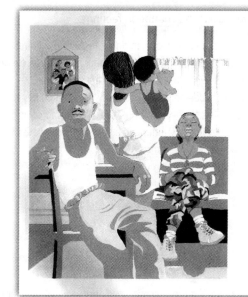

They weren't doing anything,
Mom and the baby and
Auntie Bibba and Uncle Didi,
nothing really . . .

Then,
DING DONG!
"Yoooooo hoooooo!
Yoooooo hoooooo!"

Mom looked at the door,
Uncle Didi looked at Auntie Bibba,
Auntie Bibba looked at the baby,
the baby looked at Mom.
It was . . .

Page 26: Prompt children to think, once again, about what characters are saying or thinking, drawing on what they now know about the story.

"Now that we know who's at the door—the dad—and that everyone wants to surprise him for his birthday, what do you think the characters are saying or thinking right now? Look at each person in the picture. Turn and tell your partner." Listen in to quickly assess if children are beginning to make these inferences with a bit more confidence. If possible, think back to this same prompt during the first reading to consider ways children have (or have not) revised their original ideas.

"Wow! I'm hearing so many of you change your ideas about what the characters might be saying here. Super Readers make their thinking even stronger every time they reread. The first time we read this story we thought, 'Maybe they're saying, "Who's there?"' but now that we know it's a surprise party, maybe they're saying, 'It's Daddy!' or 'He's here! Everyone hide and stay quiet so we can yell, "Surprise!"'"

Pages 30–33: Read on, stopping to prompt students to share their own ideas.

"I bet you're noticing *more* about the story and the characters from the pictures. That's one of the best parts of rereading. I'm sure you're thinking even *more*, too. Right now, turn and share the new details you're noticing and the new ideas you're having." You might then turn to the full-spread illustration across pages 32 and 33 and place it under a document camera to enlarge the picture to nudge readers to notice more details and talk about the story.

Pages 34–35: Pause to prompt children to think about the change in feelings.

"I can tell that the baby isn't feeling happy anymore. I notice he's got an angry face here." Point to the illustration on page 34. "And here," point to the illustration on page 35, "he's crying and reaching out for everyone in the family. *Why* is he so upset? Will you turn and tell your partner what you think? You can say, 'Because . . .' to explain *why*." Voice back a few sample responses you've collected from partnerships. "I heard some of you say that the baby is upset because he wants to stay up late. Thumbs up if you've felt that way before, too! And some of you said that maybe he feels sad because he's going to miss everybody when they leave. Thumbs up if you sometimes miss people in your family when they leave. He loves them *so much*, just like they love him *so much*."

Then, read to the end of the story.

AFTER YOU READ

Reread favorite pages to perform the book together.

"Let's go back and choose a few parts to read *again*. Maybe we can even perform some of the book to say the words to sound like the character or sound like the author, making our voices *sing* the words that repeat. Ready to try?" Turn back to a particular page that features some dialogue, for example, page 2. Place the text under the document camera. "Let's reread this page first. Let's all be Auntie Bibba and spread our arms out wide with a big, big smile. Then, let's talk like Auntie Bibba and say:

> '*Ooooooh!*' . . .
>
> '*I want to squeeze him,*
>
> *I want to squeeze the baby,*
>
> *I want to squeeze him*
>
> *SO MUCH!*'"

"Let's do it together!" Channel the class to recite the text with expressive voices. Then say to your students, "What else might she be saying? Turn and act it out!" Then, ask the class to suggest another part of the book to perform. You might call children up to explore different ways the character (or even narration) might sound, acting out one part a few different ways, reading in different voices with different actions. Coach readers with prompts, such as "Show the feeling." "Try it another way." "Act it out!"

SESSION 2: AS YOU READ

pp. 34–35: Pause to prompt children to think about the change in character's feelings.

"I notice that NOW the character is feeling _____. WHY? Turn and tell your partner what you think. You can say 'because _____' to explain WHY."

Shared Reading

Text Selections

> *Brown Bear, Brown Bear, What Do You See?*, by Bill Martin Jr

> Familiar song, text, or chart of your choice—for example, the alphabet chart

We chose *Brown Bear, Brown Bear, What Do You See?*, by Bill Martin Jr, because it is not only an old favorite, but it also provides children with ample practice at using and developing early reading behaviors, including one-to-one matching, using a pattern to read, building high-frequency word vocabulary, and beginning to use first letter sounds to help you read.

At this time in the year, you'll want to choose texts that are fun to read or may present patterns and rhythms to support children in reading with more accuracy and fluency. You'll still want to work on developing phonological awareness, as well. Texts like *Brown Bear, Brown Bear* offer opportunities to work on these skills. Overall, these books should be great fun and accessible, because this is a time to welcome children into the world of print and help them cross the bridge into conventional reading.

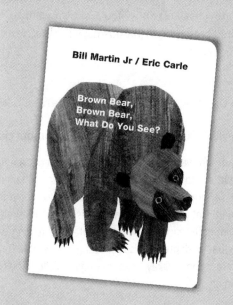

DAY ONE: Falling in Love with the Book

On this day, you'll start by introducing the book and key concepts. As you read, you will want to emphasize predicting along the way. This will draw attention to the pattern in the book as well as the words that are on the page. You will want to be sure that students are reading along with the pointer. In this unit, we are drawing more attention to the print on the page, so you will want to find every opportunity to get kids to look and think about the words.

You'll read the book, still inviting children to chime in, even on this first read. As you read, you'll want to take some time to look closely at the words with children. (Remember, you'll have all week for this work, so make careful choices about where to pause and where to keep reading.) You will want to ask kids to find words on the page, predict what some words might be (guess the covered word), as well as think about where a word starts and ends. You will also want to "share" the pointer with the students in your class. Invite selected students on various days to take turns practicing pointing under the words to help develop one-to-one matching.

DAY ONE FOCUS

✔ Introduce what the book is about.

✔ Listen to the rhymes.

✔ Use the picture to guess the word (building meaning).

✔ Work on one-to-one matching.

WARM UP: Alphabet Chart, Name Chart

Conduct a letter review with children, using two classroom charts.

You will want to warm up with some materials that students are very familiar with that you have used in past units with students. A great tool that your students should be quite familiar with is the alphabet chart. You may begin your warm-up reading by saying, "Readers, let's warm up today by reading two of the charts in our classroom. Let's begin with the alphabet chart. Get your best singing voices on and let's read together." You will want to draw attention to the letters by sharply pointing to each one with a pointer and to sing with a fluent pace. You may decide to pause on key letters to make sure that students are also following the pointer. Then you could also add in voiceovers such as "Don't read ahead. The pointer is on *g*. Okay, keep on singing. Follow the pointer," and "Did we say, /p/? Is the pointer on *p?* Great, let's keep reading."

After you have read the chart, you may decide to compliment your class and say, "What beautiful singing voices, and great job following the pointer. I am wondering, who can find the letter *a* on our chart? Sara, can you come up quickly and touch it? Do we agree? Is that *a?* Yes. Who can find the letter *p*, like pppp/ig? Thanks, Carl. We agree? Yes, there is the pig in the picture. That is a *p*. What letter do you want me to find? How about *d?* That is a tricky one. Dddd/og. Mmm, . . . here?" Here, you may purposefully point to the fish. Your class will undoubtedly correct you! This will be a great opportunity to assess what your students know, to see who is able to follow along, and to also notice who can work, not just "in context" but "out of context" as well.

You can repeat the same type of work with another wall chart in your classroom, the name chart. You may say to your class, "Let's see if we can read all the names in our class as well. Let's read the name chart." Then ask for a few volunteers to find some names to point to on the chart. "Whose name starts with an *m?*" and "Who can find Fernando's name?" Here you are working similar skills, just in a different material.

BOOK INTRODUCTION AND FIRST READING: *Brown Bear, Brown Bear, What Do You See?*, by Bill Martin Jr

Give a book introduction to provide the gist of the story and entice readers.

You will, of course, want to recruit the class to join in a shared reading of this book. You will want not only to do some of the early reading behaviors like talking about the cover and doing a picture walk of the first few pages, but you will want to talk about what this book is about and get your class to think early on about the pattern that they will find. You may say, "We are going to find that these animals are looking at one another. I wonder, what kinds of animals are we going to find? Let's see!"

As you read, you will want to guess a couple of words that are covered up.

Choose words that relate to the pattern of the book as well as words children can solve by using the picture (and the meaning of the text/pattern) to help them "guess the covered word." For example, you might select *red* to cover. When you come to the covered word, listen to what your kids do. See if they just say, "Red." If so, ask, "How do you know? Oh! It is a red bird. Rrrrr/ed. Starts with an *r*. Let's look! 'Red!' Let's keep reading." Repeat this with a different word such as *dog*. Choose three or four words to do this with during the first reading.

Find at least one place to stop and turn and talk about the story.

You might say, "I wonder what animal is going to be next *and* what color it will be?" You will also invite kids to use their bodies to create gestures with parts of the text: "Can we read that again, the 'looking at me' part? This time, let's point to our eyes for *looking* and use our thumbs to point at ourselves for *me!*"

REREADING WITH A FOCUS

Reread all (or part) of *Brown Bear, Brown Bear*, emphasizing different things readers do each time.

Once you have read through the entire text, reread the story at least once or twice, to offer additional practice with the skills you're supporting kindergartners to use independently. On your first focused rereading, for example, you may highlight one-to-one matching. You may even invite a reader in your class to be the pointer for a couple of pages, and then switch to another student. You will want to emphasize how to point *under* the words and to keep the pointer moving, left to right. You will want to emphasize to the readers not to "read ahead" of the pointer. You will want to stop the children to make sure that what they are reading are the words that the pointer is under!

You may also take the pointer and read a page with your students and ask, "Who can find the word *cat?*" or "Who can find the word *me?*" This will not only help build high-frequency word recognition, such as the word *me*, but it also will help students focus on the concept of a word and begin to use letters and sounds to locate words on the page.

Use this rereading as a formative assessment to find out what words students recognize automatically, how they are doing with one-to-one matching, and what they know about letters and sounds.

AFTER READING

Conduct a wrap-up activity at the end of the book, such as a class retell of the book. Then teach your kids how they too can make a similar book, but with the kids in the classroom.

After you read, you may want to say your students, "So, let's see. At the end of that story, were the animals real? Or were the children pretending to be animals? Let's try to remember all the animals that were looking at the teacher! Turn to your partner and name as many as you can. Use your fingers to count how many you can remember.

"Wow, you all remembered, almost *all* of them! Fantastic. I thought we could make our *own* book about the kids in our classroom. We can use the names in our class, instead of animals." I pointed to the name chart. "I will write names in these blank spaces." I showed them a laminated sentence strip that I had made:

____, ____, what do you see? I see _____ looking at me!

"Then we can read about our class looking at each other! Let's try it! Beth, will you choose a name off of the name chart?" I wrote Beth's name in the first two blank spaces.

"Sara!" she chose.

"Great, now I will write Sara's name in the empty blank space, here. Can you all shout out the letters in Sara's name?" Record the letters as kids spell it out loud. "Thank you for that help. Now, let's read."

Beth, Beth, what do you see? I see Sara looking at me!

"So much fun! Now, quickly Sara, choose a new name, from our name chart." I erased Beth's and Sara's names. I wrote Sara's name in the first two blank spaces.

"Carl!" she shouted.

"Wonderful. Everyone, cheer out the letters in Carl's name!" As they shouted I wrote his name in the last blank space. "And now let's read!"

Sara, Sara, what do you see? I see Carl, looking at me!

On this day, you'll reread the book with a focus on *looking closely* at the pictures as well as *using* them to help solve words on the page. This is a wonderful time to work on building oral language skills and the ability to talk about what you see on the page. This will help to build meaning in texts and better understanding.

In this unit of study you are bringing kids closer and closer to conventional reading. This is a wonderful opportunity to work on developing using the sources of information—meaning, structure, visual (MSV)—at the most rudimentary stage. Many of your students are learning what a word is and working on one-to-one matching. They are also beginning to use pictures to help them think about what a word might be. They are beginning to use many letters to record the sounds that they hear in writing. In reading they are beginning to notice and use initial letters to help think about what a word might be. At this earliest stage of reading, they are also beginning to use patterns to help them read words. All of these things you can reinforce through shared reading.

WARM UP: A Familiar Text

Quickly reread a familiar text (i.e., a poem, song, chant, chart, the word wall) to build confidence and excitement and get voices ready.

You will want to warm up your reader by rereading some sort of familiar chart, song, or nursery rhyme. You will also want to give students more of a role in leading this reading. Perhaps you will invite a student to be the pointer as you read the name chart. You might say, "Danika, come up and be our pointer. Remember, one tap for each name. Let's read, following Danika's pointer!" As the class reads together, in unison, you will want to periodically voice over reminders such as "Check the picture first. Who is this name going to be?" "Are you sure it's Sara? How do we know? I see her picture *and* the letter *s* for *Sara*!" "Is this *Tristan* or *Tracy*? Let's check the picture and make sure."

After reading across the chart, you may want to play a game with the names, coaching kids to read the names without picture support, relying on visual information, especially the first letter. This extension will give students more practice. You may begin explaining the game by saying, "Can I show you what I have in my hands? I have six names in my hand on these note cards. I will put one in the pocket chart, and you can think about *whose* name it is. Then, we will match the name with our chart. When you have an idea, put your finger on your lips and your other thumb on your knee. Don't shout it out! Ready?"

Hold up one student's name and then say, "I hear kids saying the /g/ sound. I see kids checking the name chart for letters. I see kids pointing to the picture. Sara, come on up. If you agree with where she matches the name, put two thumbs up. If you disagree, put two thumbs sideways." Continue in this quick fashion with five other names and then reread the name chart one more time.

DAY TWO FOCUS

✔ Develop early concepts about print, language structure, phonological awareness (rhyming and word play), and of course, comprehension.

✔ Study pictures to notice more details.

✔ Practice looking at pictures and using them to help find words.

SECOND READING: *Brown Bear, Brown Bear, What Do You See?*

Purple Cat,
Purple Cat,
What do you see?

I see a white dog
looking at me.

As you read today, you'll place an emphasis on studying the pictures.

You might start by saying, "Super Readers, let's reread *Brown Bear, Brown Bear*. As we read, let's stop and study the pictures on the pages and try to say all the things that we see!"

Help your students study the pictures and look around at the different parts of the animals. After you all read the first page you might say, "Let's look at this bear and say all the things you see!" Kids might notice four paws, two ears, and a black nose.

Then you might add on by saying, "Let's zoom in closely here. Look at those paws. I see long sharp nails! Let's read the page again and get ready for what is next." After the class rereads the page you might say, "So what are we going to see? Let's see if you are right." Then, turn the page to confirm the prediction and read the page together.

Cover a few of the words, encouraging children to use the picture and the pattern to read.

You may begin to mask the noun in the book, so that students use the picture to help them think about what word it might be. Choose three nouns, especially animals that are well known to your class such as the duck, horse, and frog. Prompt your kids to figure it out. "What might this word be? Check the picture. Let's reread and see if that would make sense. It does! Now, what letter will see at the beginning of the word if it is /d/uck?" Over exaggerate the sound /d/. Let's check. It is! Let's keep reading."

You also might cover the color word, such as purple or white. If you do, you might prompt kids in this way: "Uh-oh. Let's look at the picture and think about this first word. I see a cat. I see a purple cat. Will it be cat or purple cat? Let's remember the pattern of the book. Purple? Let's see if we see the letter that makes the /p/ sound at the beginning. We do! Purple! Let's read this page together!"

AFTER READING

Engage children in seeing and saying additional things about the animals in the book.

You will want to have your students talk about the animals in the book and the things that they now know about them. Then you will want to help your kids say more about the pages. You might say, "Let's look more carefully at the green frog page. Let's see if we can notice more things in the picture that we can say about the frog." Point to a few parts in the picture and then call on students to say things to the whole class about what they now see and notice. Students may say things like "The green frog has webbed feet," and "He doesn't want the cat to eat him, so he's going to jump, jump away!"

After students have said a couple of things about one page, prompt them to talk about a new page. You may say, "Does anyone else have something to say about the frog or another animal?"

DAY THREE: Word Play

On this day, you'll focus on word study activities relevant to the work students need at these levels, primarily phonological awareness. This day might look more like inquiry, studying particular word study concepts and hunting for words or features. Word study includes several important concepts: concepts about print (at the book and the word level), phonological awareness, phonics, and high-frequency word recognition. The power of shared reading is that it gives all kids access to print at their level of understanding. So while some kids will be developing the concept of one-to-one matching, others may be recognizing high-frequency words. At this point in the year, you might choose to have your kindergartners play with rhyming words, hunt for letters, or clap syllables.

DAY THREE FOCUS

✔ Develop phonological awareness.

✔ Highlight high-frequency words.

✔ Play with rhyme.

WARM UP: A Familiar Text

Quickly reread a familiar text to build confidence and excitement and get voices ready.

You may want to start with the name chart and then launch into reading the poem "I Like to Play." Begin to sing the poem to the tune of "Happy Birthday."

I Like to Play

I like to play with you.

I like to play with you.

I like to play with _____.

I like to play with you.

Consider having the class names on index cards (with accompanying photos if possible). Invite a student to come up to the front and choose a name and place it in the blank spot for everybody to read (possibly in a pocket chart). Then have the student lead the class in reading and singing by holding the pointer.

You may decide to repeat this with five or six other names.

THIRD READING: *Brown Bear, Brown Bear, What Do You See?*

Continue to support students' growing understanding of print concepts and phonological awareness.

For example, you might pause at the end of a page and say, "Hmm, . . . where is the word *duck*? Let's say the word /d/ uck. What do we hear at the beginning? /D/! Let's find *duck*." Ask one of your students to come up, and then ask the other students to listen and see if they agree. If they do, they may indicate it by putting a thumb on their knee. Then you might prompt them to think about if they have seen this somewhere else. Afterward you might say, "I am done reading this line. Where should I move my pointer?" This will help to reinforce skills like "return sweep."

Develop students' phonemic awareness and have them recognize rhyming words.

You might say as you are rereading, "Let's read this page and listen for two words that rhyme. Then let's put a Wiki Stix around them and notice what they look like and how they sound."

Highlight familiar word wall words as you read.

You might start by saying, "Let's look at our class word wall and remember the snap words we've learned so far. Read them with me!" After reading these words in isolation, from a nearby word wall or a pocket chart, invite students to hunt for them in the class shared text. You might say, "If you spot one of our snap words in *Brown Bear, Brown Bear*, snap your fingers! Then, we can stop and put highlighting tape to make those words pop!"

AFTER READING

Play a quick rhyming game with students, choosing different words to fill in the rhyme.

You might choose to continue playing with rhyme by singing a rhyming song such as "Five Little Ducks" or a song that kids can manipulate, inserting words to fill in the rhyme. For example, you might sing, "Down by the Bay" to create silly rhymes across verses. You might also choose to sing "The Name Game" to create nonsense words as you rhyme with each child's name: "Katie, Katie, bo-batie. Banana-fana fo-fatie. Fee-fi-mo-matie . . . Katie!"

On this day, you'll want to focus on fluency, helping children to read more smoothly, automatically, and with appropriate rate, prosody, and intonation, as well as begin to attend to punctuation.

WARM UP: A Familiar Text

Quickly reread a familiar text to build confidence and excitement and get voices ready.

"I Like to Play" offers a variety of ways for children to build confidence, excitement, and fluency. You may decide to let your voice fall so that students do the work of carrying the rhythm, reading with greater fluency as you swap in a different child's name for each rereading of the poem.

FOURTH READING: *Brown Bear, Brown Bear, What Do You See?*

While reading with fluency and expression, invite children to join you in putting stress on certain words or phrases (prosody).

You might demonstrate reading in a way that emphasizes the end rhyme on each page of the book. You may even invite kids to clap once as they read the last word of each sentence as a way to signify the rhyme and beat. For example, you might read (and clap) along with the children, "Brown Bear, Brown Bear, What do you *see* (clap!)? I see a red bird looking at *me* (clap!)." You might go on to demonstrate how to stress other words as you read on, such as *you* and *I*, as in the line, "Yellow Duck, Yellow Duck, What do *you* see? *I* see a blue horse looking at me." Choose places to let your voice drop, pushing the class to take a bigger role in the choral reading, removing the support of your voice to move kids toward more independence with fluency and expression.

Together, pause to act out parts of the book, and make your voices sound like that of the character or narrator.

You might consider assigning different roles to different groups of children around the meeting area. You could say, "This group here, you'll be the blue horse. When we get to that page, I want *your* voices to rise up louder. Make your reading voice sound like the horse talking."

Pay attention to punctuation and think about how to make your reading voice match.

Take a moment to scan the page for punctuation marks, focusing on end punctuation rather than commas. You might say, "Oh! I spy a period at the end of this sentence. We'll need to

Yellow Duck,
Yellow Duck,
What do you see?

I see a blue horse
looking at me.

make sure to *stop* and take a breath before we read on. Ready? Let's read." You might highlight the punctuation to make it pop off the page so readers can grow to be more accountable to attending to these cues when reading.

AFTER READING

Engage the class in making rhyming words, both real and nonsense.

You could play a quick rhyming game with students, choosing a few words from the book to use. For example, "Let's see if we can make lots of rhyming words with *splash*." You might even create a signal for when you rhyme with real words and another signal for when you rhyme with nonsense words. "Readers, when we rhyme, sometimes we think of real words and sometimes we make up silly words. When we say a real word, put your finger on your nose. When we say a silly word, put your finger on your shoulder."

DAY FIVE: Extending the Text

On this, your final day with the shared text, you'll put it all together, encouraging children to read as independently as they can. You'll also take the time to extend the text, perhaps through interactive writing, drama, or talking about the book. Small copies of the book can then be made available for children to read on their own, during reading workshop, as well as any interactive writing you create.

WARM UP: A Familiar Text

Quickly reread a familiar text to build confidence and excitement and get voices ready.

You might want to prepare an "I Can Read" chart and lead the class in a quick, rallying chant. It might go like this:

> I can read. I can read. I can read, read, READ!
>
> I can read books. Yes, I can!
>
> I can read signs. Yes, I can!
>
> I can read labels. Yes, I can!
>
> I can read names. Yes, I can!
>
> I can read charts. Yes, I can!
>
> I can read songs. Yes, I can!
>
> I can read. I can read. I can read, read, READ!

DAY FIVE FOCUS

✔ Orchestrate strategies learned across the week.

✔ Extend comprehension.

FIFTH READING: *Brown Bear, Brown Bear, What Do You See?*

Allow students' reading voices to outshine your own, perhaps letting your voice drop entirely.

Remind readers to use strategies you've been building across the week. You might invite specific students to turn the pages, or point crisply under words as the class reads along. Prompt students to problem solve if they get stuck. "Use the picture to remember how this part goes. What might the words say here?" "Remember the pattern." "Let's reread that and match our voices!"

AFTER READING

Engage the class in a discussion about the characters.

You might think about how each animal is feeling across the book, imagining what they're thinking about the other animals. Students could take on voices to act out each part, trying it several ways and deciding which fits best.

Additional opportunities to act out the story are a great way to deepen students' comprehension of texts and support language development. During choice time, you could provide materials for students to make simple props or puppets. They could use these to act out the story as they turn the pages of the book.

You might also do interactive writing connected to the text.

For example, you might label details in the pictures or add speech bubbles across different pages. You might label each animal's attributes, such as "pointy beak" and "long wing." To add speech bubbles across pages you might prompt children to consider what different characters are saying or thinking. You might prompt, "What do you think Red Bird is thinking about Yellow Duck? Let's add a speech bubble." Similarly, you might add a page or change the ending.

Separately, you may choose to do some shared writing with your students to support language and writing development, composing and recording a letter to the characters or the author. You could also reconstruct the text, manipulating parts such as changing the animals or the colors. You might prepare index cards with all the repeating words of the text and, using a pocket chart, have children help you construct the lines, inserting new characters, perhaps "Pink Unicorn, Pink Unicorn, what do you see?" You'll want to place copies of any shared or interactive writing you do in students' book baggies, so they can read these teacher-supported materials independently during reading workshop.